Beginnings

Jim Branch

This book consists of two distinct parts. **Part one** involves time <u>together</u> (once or twice a week) with a leader, mentor, pastor, or older friend. And **part two** (starting on page 23) involves spending daily time <u>alone</u> with God, one-on-one, just you and Him. Both should be started the first couple of days after you begin your journey with Jesus; it will be a good way to set the tone for this new life with Him.

Part One
(To be done with your leader, mentor, etc.)

Welcome to God's Family

How incredibly exciting it is that you have begun this new relationship with Jesus! I am so glad that God has placed His hand on you and drawn you to Himself. And as glad as I am about you beginning this new adventure with Jesus, my excitement is nothing compared to the excitement of those who know you well and love you deeply; those who have been praying and hoping and longing for this day to come—the day when you would trust Jesus with all of your heart, soul, and life. Seeing you in this place has long been one of the deepest desires of their hearts; this place of knowing, understanding, and receiving God's great love and deep affection for you.

But no matter how excited those around you are, their excitement pales in comparison to the excitement that is in God's own heart right now about your coming home to Him—your true home. There are many great pictures of this in the Bible, but maybe none sweeter than the one in Zephaniah 3:16-17 where it tells us that God is so delighted to be in relationship with us that it brings a song to his lips and joy to His heart. Is that not INCREDIBLE! The God of the universe is so pleased that you have come into a relationship with Him that He bursts into song.

Cheer up! Don't be afraid! For the Lord your God has arrived to live among you. He is a mighty savior. He will rejoice over you with great gladness. With his love, he will calm all your fears. He will exult over you by singing a happy song. (Zephaniah 3:16-17)

Knowing and following Him is a lifelong process—one that is not easy and will not make all of your problems go away. But it is, nonetheless, a process that offers you a real relationship with the Living God—one that will bring a richness and a peace; a fullness and a depth to your life that you have never imagined.

One: Loved by God

Ultimately the adventure you have just begun is about getting to know, and falling more and more in love with Jesus. And like any other relationship, building it takes time and intention. As we get to know Jesus, we get to know his heart for us. And as we get to know his heart for us, we come to understand how deeply we are loved. And more than anything else, the life of faith is a life of love—God's incredible love for us and our love (in response) for him. It is the knowledge of his love and affection that will change everything—a knowledge of the heart rather than just the head. When we begin to understand the extravagance of God's love, our hearts are completely captured by love for him in return. When we taste his great affection it will completely reorder our affections.

In John 3:16 God gives us a brief glimpse at this amazing love. A love so great that He gave his own son for us—that we might spend eternity with the Lover of our souls. Nothing else in all of Scripture is more important to understand than this. If we can begin to grasp the height and depth and breadth of His love for us, everything else will fall into place.

Do you know how deeply you are loved by the God who made you? His love for you is beyond limits. His love for you is without measure. His love for you cannot be overstated. His love for you is total and complete. His love for you will never fail.

Turn to John 3:16 in your Bible and read it together.

Now spend some time together talking about the following questions: *What has been your experience with God to this point in your life? What is it that has convinced you to begin a relationship with Him? Where do you think you go from here? What are you most excited about? What fears do you have?*

Two: Made in His image

Read:
Psalm 139:13-16
*Oh yes, you shaped me first inside, then out; you
formed me in my mother's womb. I thank you High
God—you're breathtaking! Body and soul, I am
marvelously made! I worship in adoration—what a
creation!* (The Message)

Ephesians 2:10
For we are God's masterpiece. (NLT)

Did you know that you were made by the God of all
creation? That's right, before the foundations of the
world were put into place, you were an idea—a beautiful
thought—in the mind and heart of God, one that brought
a smile to His lips and joy to His heart. In fact, He
dreamt you into being; you are the work of his wild
imagination and wonderfully creative hands. You are
His masterpiece.

Read:
Genesis 1:26-27
[26] *Then God said, "Let us make man in our image, in
our likeness, and let them rule over the fish of the sea
and the birds of the air, over the livestock, over all the
earth, and over all the creatures that move along the
ground."*
[27] *So God created man in his own image,
in the image of God he created him;
male and female he created them.(NIV)*

Did you know that you were actually made in God's very
image? God created all the other parts of this amazing
universe and world, and then he did something totally
unique, something he had not done before. He made us
in His image. He made us to be like Him in some unique

and mysterious way that had not occurred up to this point in the story of creation. We are made in the very image of God. What exactly does that mean?

A wise saint of old once said that we were "created out of the laughter of the Trinity." In other words, we were created out of an incredible outpouring of love that was going on in the very heart of God. Somehow God (Father, Son, and Holy Spirit) was so filled with love that He couldn't contain Himself and decided to create. And the crown jewel of that creation would be us—men and women—who were made in such a way that we can share in this love like nothing else in all creation is able to. God made us—you and me—for relationship with Himself!!! Is that not unbelievable? God made us to love us...and to be loved by us.

Read:
Ephesians 3:14-19

When I think of the wisdom and scope of God's plan, I fall to my knees and pray to the Father, the Creator of everything in heaven and on earth. I pray that from his glorious, unlimited resources he will give you mighty inner strength through his Holy Spirit. And I pray that Christ will be more and more at home in your hearts as you trust in him. May your roots go down deep into the soil of God's marvelous love. And may you have the power to understand, as all God's people should, how wide, how long, how high, and how deep his love really is. May you experience the love of Christ, though it is so great you will never fully understand it. Then you will be filled with the fullness of life and power that comes from God. (NLT)

Psalm 149:4

For the Lord takes delight in his people; he crowns the humble with salvation.

God loves us deeply. In fact, He delights in us. His love for us is the thing that is meant to give us our deepest and truest sense of joy and identity. If we are ever tempted to doubt our worth or our value, all we have to do is look at the immense love and delight that God has in His heart for us and be convinced once again that we are priceless to the One who made us uniquely and loves us dearly. Did you know that you bring great joy and delight to the heart of God?

Read:
Romans 8:35-39
 35 Who shall separate us from the love of Christ? Shall trouble or hardship or persecution or famine or nakedness or danger or sword? 36 As it is written:

> *"For your sake we face death all day long;*
> *we are considered as sheep to be slaughtered."*

 37 No, in all these things we are more than conquerors through him who loved us. 38 For I am convinced that neither death nor life, neither angels nor demons, neither the present nor the future, nor any powers, 39 neither height nor depth, nor anything else in all creation, will be able to separate us from the love of God that is in Christ Jesus our Lord.

Colossians 2:6-7
 6 And now, just as you accepted Christ Jesus as your Lord, you must continue to follow him. 7 Let your roots grow down into him, and let your lives be built on him. Then your faith will grow strong in the truth you were taught, and you will overflow with thankfulness. (NLT)

The bottom line is that God loves you with a love that knows no limits, and that nothing can ever separate you from His everlasting love. Our challenge is to become more and more *convinced* of this love with each passing day, and to fall more and more deeply in love with Him. Growing in this love relationship with Him is the true essence of the Christian life.

Questions for Discussion and Reflection:
What does it mean for you to have a loving relationship with God? Is this a new thought? How do you feel about it? How does it make you feel that you are so incredibly loved by God? What does it mean that you were made in God's image? Is it hard to believe that God delights in you? Why or why not? What does all of this mean for your self-worth?

Three: Our images of God

How we see God is extremely important. In fact, it might be one of the most important things about us. How we see God—our images of Him—determine so much about our belief, and ultimately about how we live our lives.

We all have our own set of thoughts and images; our own pictures about what we truly believe God to be like. Some of these images are based on fact and some of them just based on misguided comments and painful experiences. These images come from numerous sources: our family, our childhood experiences, books, television, movies, friends, etc. Paying attention to these images is important because they determine, to a large degree, what we believe about God and how we choose to relate to him—not to mention how we think He will relate to us. The first step in this process is identifying our own thoughts and images of God. What pictures or images do you have of Him?

Exercise: *Take a few minutes and write down (or draw) pictures or images that you might have of God. After you are finished, talk about these images with your mentor/leader (or another older Christian adult in your life). Example: your pictures of God might be...an old man in the sky, someone distant and uninvolved, a rule maker, an over- protective parent, someone to steal your fun, etc.*

The next step is to determine, "Where did these pictures or images come from?"

Exercise II: *Take the pictures of God you came up with and try to trace them to their source. How accurate do you think these images of God really are?*

The final step is to consider the question, "How do you think God might be different from these pictures or images you have of Him?"

Exercise III: *Spend some time writing in your journal about the following question, "How has what you have heard about God recently (from camp, club, friends, church, or wherever) been different from the pictures of God you have always had?" And then spend some time talking about that with your leader/mentor.*

Read:
Colossians 1:15
Christ is the visible image of the invisible God. He existed before anything was created and is supreme over all creation. (NLT)

Hebrews 1:3
The Son is the radiance of God's glory and the exact representation of his being, sustaining all things by his powerful word.

Ultimately Jesus is the most accurate picture we have of God. He is the visible, tangible image of the invisible God. If we want to know what God is like, we must look at Jesus—God's visible expression.

Four: How God Sees Us

How do you think God sees you?

Exercise: Write down some words that you think best describe how God sees you. Why do you think that?

The Bible is filled with example after example of how God really sees us. Each one of these pictures has unique qualities and characteristics about it that show us, to one degree or another, one particular way that God sees us. Pay special attention to these characteristics in the following verses and describe the special qualities of each.

Read: John 10:1-18 - Sheep with a Shepherd
(Look it up in your Bible)

We are sheep under his tender care and direction. What are the qualities of sheep and how are we like them spiritually? What are the qualities of a shepherd and how does he see the sheep? What do you think God is trying to say about our relationship with Him in these verses?

Read: John 15:13-17 – Friends of God

We are His friends that He lays down His life for. What are the qualities of true friendship? What is significant about Jesus calling us his friends? What does this picture tell you about our relationship with him?

Read: Luke 15:11-32 - His Beloved Children

We are His beloved children—sons and daughters of God—and He is our loving Father. What are the qualities of a really good father/child relationship? What are the qualities you have always hoped for in a father? How do you think a loving father looks at his children?

What does this picture tell you about how God sees you?

Read: Isaiah 62:5 - His Beautiful Bride

We are His bride. What does a groom's face look like when he sees his Bride coming down the aisle? What do you think is in his heart? What are the qualities of a passionately loving relationship? What does this picture tell you about how God sees you?

Read: Ephesians 1:7-8 - Forgiven and Redeemed

We are forgiven and redeemed. To be redeemed means to be "bought back out of slavery." Because of our sin—our turning away from God to our own ways and agendas—we were slaves to sin, but now God has bought us back for himself by the ransom of His very life. And now we belong to Him.
　　How does it make you feel to know that you are completely forgiven by God? What was the price involved in God offering you this forgiveness? What does the word "redeemed" mean to you? What have you been redeemed from? What have you been redeemed for? What does this picture tell you about how God sees you?

Five: Living Life in Christ

Read:
Acts 2:37-47
　　37 Now when they heard this they were cut to the heart, and said to Peter and the rest of the apostles, "Brothers, what shall we do?" 38 And Peter said to them, "Repent and be baptized every one of you in the name of Jesus Christ for the forgiveness of your sins, and you will receive the gift of the Holy Spirit. 39 For the promise is for you and for your children and for all who are far off,

*everyone whom the Lord our God calls to himself." [40]
And with many other words he bore witness and
continued to exhort them, saying, "Save yourselves from
this crooked generation." [41] So those who received his
word were baptized, and there were added that day
about three thousand souls.*

*[42] And they devoted themselves to the apostles'
teaching and the fellowship, to the breaking of bread and
the prayers. [43] And awe came upon every soul, and
many wonders and signs were being done through the
apostles. [44] And all who believed were together and had
all things in common. [45] And they were selling their
possessions and belongings and distributing the
proceeds to all, as any had need. [46] And day by day,
attending the temple together and breaking bread in their
homes, they received their food with glad and generous
hearts, [47] praising God and having favor with all the
people. And the Lord added to their number day by day
those who were being saved. (ESV)*

It is a key moment in the lives of Jesus' early followers.
He has died on the cross, risen from the grave,
appeared to the disciples several times over a forty day
period, and now ascended back to heaven. The Holy
Spirit has just been poured out upon them, and for the
very first time they get to stand in the middle of the city in
which all of this took place and tell the story. And what
an incredible story it is! So Peter stands and addresses
the crowd, telling them the beautiful story of Jesus; much
like the one you probably heard recently.

When he had finished his message, we are told that
the people were *cut to the heart.* What a great phrase
describing the mysterious nature of what happened
within them. This message—about the power and love of
Jesus—simply does something deeply within them (and
us): something that is real, something that is powerful,
something that is life-changing. And did you notice their
response? Did you see what happens next? They ask a
question. A question very similar to the one you may be
asking yourself right now as you embark on this new and

exciting life adventure: *Brothers, what shall we do?* In other words, *"What in the world do I do now?"*

Luckily we are not left in the dark to answer this question completely on our own. In fact, these very verses begin to give us a good idea of what it looks like to begin a life with Jesus, to start building a relationship with Him. And ultimately, that is exactly what we're talking about; living life with God, developing a wonderfully intimate friendship with the One who made us for relationship with Himself. So, where do we begin?

Well, the first thing Peter tells them is that they must **repent**. That might be a word you are either not familiar with or drawn to, but is actually a beautiful word, meaning "to change one's mind." The image it creates is a deep change of heart and mind that leads to a new direction in our lives. We go from following our own leading, to following Jesus. Thus, to repent means *to turn*. Peter is telling them that the first thing they must do is *turn*; *turn* to God, not just once, but always and again. You see, what God most wants for us is not just a moment when we stand and "say so" but a life in which we grow in love for and devotion to Him. He wants us to live life *with* Him, and living life *with* Him involves a constant *turning*. Turning to Him initially in faith to begin our relationship with Him, and turning to Him regularly after that to deepen our relationship with Him.

It is kind of like the difference between a wedding and a marriage. God longs for that moment when we finally say to Him "I do" and enter into this intimate relationship with Him (wedding). But He also wants what comes after, a wonderfully intimate, growing love relationship for the rest of our lives (marriage)—as well as the rest of eternity. After all, what good is a wedding day without a wonderful marriage that follows? As a matter of fact, if you were to ask me about my relationship with my sweet wife, I would definitely tell you about the incredible day we were married, but much more than that, I would tell you about the wonderful life and marriage we have shared since that day (for the last 30+ years). What God really wants with each of us is a marriage, not just a wedding.

So what does this life with God look like? Well if we continue to read Acts 2, we begin to see a beautiful picture of that. In fact, after Peter's message that day, the people began to order their lives in a certain way, in order to nurture this new-found relationship with Jesus. This ordering specifically involved four things that they *devoted themselves to*. The word *devoted* that is used here literally means *to be strong toward*. They decided that, in order to nurture this new life they had just begun, there were four things they needed to be *strong toward*: the apostle's teaching, the fellowship, the breaking of the bread, and the prayers. These four elements were essential to growing their new life with Jesus, so much so that they made sure to create space for each of these things daily. And these four daily practices not only offered them a great framework for ordering their spiritual journey with Jesus, but they also do the same for us.

Exercise: Take a look at Acts 2:37-47 with your leader. What words or images are you most drawn to? Why? What things marked the new believer's life with Jesus? What marked their life with each other? Now take each one of the four elements of their common life mentioned in verse 42 and talk with your leader about how each one can become a part of your own journey.

Over the next few meetings we will take a look together at each of these four essential elements to living life with Jesus.

Six: The Apostle's Teaching or God's Word

As in any relationship, one of the most important parts is simply getting to know one another. We typically do this by spending time together; talking and listening, and just *being with* each other. This new-found relationship with God is no different; in order for it to grow in intimacy, depth, and quality we must get to know each other.

Therefore, it is really important each day to set aside time to be with God and begin to get to know who He is and what He is like, as well as to listen to what He has to say. One key factor in doing this is spending daily time in God's Word. God's Word, the Bible, is the most tangible way we have to hear from God and to see what He is like. Therefore, it is important that we not just read the Bible, but actually listen to what it has to say—or better yet what God has to say through it—to us.

I have a friend named Robert that I love dearly, and who I know dearly loves me. From time to time Robert will write me a letter. Well, because of his unique handwriting and the fact that he always puts a particular little symbol on the envelope to let me know he is praying for me, I always can tell, from the very moment I pull the letter out of the mailbox, exactly who it is from. So, in my excitement, I take the letter into the house and find a quiet place where I know I will not be interrupted, and I read the letter from cover to cover. I read it slowly, wanting to take everything in. I read every line. I read between the lines. In fact, if I read it slowly enough I can almost hear his voice, as I read the words he has written especially for (or more accurately *to*) me. In fact, when I am done, I will often go back and read the whole letter again…and maybe even again. Why? Because I know his heart for me. Because I know that whatever words are contained in this letter are specifically chosen for me and are spoken to me out of love and care.

That's the way it is with God's Word as well. We have to train ourselves to read it a certain way. We have to train ourselves to listen to His voice and to see His face in the midst of the words, knowing that within it there is a Word spoken especially for us. Therefore, we must read it slowly, paying attention to every little detail, savoring it, chewing on it over and over again until we have gotten all the flavor out of it that He intended for us to get. And as we read God's Word like this each and every day, something wonderfully mysterious happens. Slowly, over time, we begin to hear His voice in the words of scripture, and we actually begin to get to know Him better and better.

So if you haven't already, start today. That's exactly what the second half of this book is all about; getting to know God. And we get to know God, by getting to know Jesus, the visible expression (image) of the invisible God. So start in the book of John (or Mark) and get to know Jesus. Listen to His words, look at His actions, see how He treats people, be amazed at how He loves people. And, most of all, be completely captured by the depths of His love for you.

Read:
Hebrews 4:12-13; 2 Timothy 3:16; Psalm 119:9-16,105

Exercise: Begin to write down what God is saying to you through His Word in a journal or notebook. Begin with these verses. What do they say to you about the value of God's Word?

Now talk about the following questions. What do these verses say about God's Word? What do they say about its role in our lives?

Exercise: Read Isaiah 55
As you read, try not just to read the words, but to actually listen to what God is saying to you through them. This type of reading is different from the way you might typically read a school book—for information. This type of reading is done for *formation*—to listen to the words with great attentiveness to what God is saying to you and how He might want it to take shape (or *form)* in your life. Reading in this way involves a certain rhythm:

reading, reflecting, responding, and resting. It is kind of like learning the steps to a wonderful dance; once they become a part of you, they can be a life-giving way of dancing with God and His Word.

Now answer these questions in your journal and talk about them with your leader:

What does it mean to listen to God's voice as you read his Word? What did God say to you through His Word today?

Seven: The Fellowship

Life with Jesus was never meant to be lived alone, but always in community. Therefore, surrounding yourself with a community of friends that are committed to walking the same journey with Jesus that you are is absolutely essential.

Read:
Ecclesiastes 4:9-12

What do these verses say about the value and function of community? In what ways can you see "two being better than one" as you journey together with Jesus?

Read:
Hebrews 10:19-25

What do these verses say about the role of community in the life of faith? What would it look like to be a part of a group that is intentional about all of these things?

Exercise: If you are meeting with a group, spend some time talking with each other about how these things will be a part of your commitment to each other.

If you are not meeting in a group, spend a little time with your leader talking about the *who, how,* and *where* of starting a group.

Eight: The Breaking of the Bread

Whenever the article "the" appears in front of the words *breaking of the bread* in Scripture, it is talking about something far more than merely sharing a meal together. In fact a few verses after this phrase is used in Acts, the writer goes on to say that they often gathered in homes to eat together (Acts 2:46). *The* Breaking of the Bread, however, refers to something different altogether. It refers to the regular practice of the early believers of gathering to remember the Lord's death, just the way he told them to in the gospels (Matthew 26:26-30, Mark 14:22-26, Luke 22:19-20). This regular gathering is frequently called the Eucharist, or the Lord's Supper, and is celebrated by communities of believers throughout the world. These communities (churches) are an essential part of living life with Jesus. As you begin this journey, it is of utmost importance that you find one of these bodies and begin to walk in life and faith with them. They will be a guide and a support, a source of wisdom and direction, a place of connection and deep communion as you walk this journey together with Jesus.

A Story: I became a Christian at Windy Gap in November of my senior year of high school. Up until that time, I had very little exposure to, or experience of, the church. Of course I had been a time or two in my childhood, but nothing that made any lasting impact on my life at all—unless it was a little negative. So when I trusted Jesus at Windy Gap I was entering a whole new world in every way imaginable. As a result of that, my YL leader told me that he thought it would be a good idea if I got involved in a church once I got home from camp. So when we returned I began considering where I might go. I knew that one of my really good childhood friends went to a church very near my house, so I decided to start with that one. Cedar Springs Presbyterian…sounded as good as any. So in early November of 1977 I started going to that big church down the street from my house—and it was like I'd found a home. The way I was embraced and welcomed and nurtured and taught just seemed to fit who I was, and what I needed, so well at that point in my life that I soon became a member. Well, that was 35+ years ago…and I am still a member of that same church. It truly has been a spiritual home. The men and women of that church have taken me in as their own and have invested in my life and my marriage and my ministry for 35 years. When I was trying to make career decisions in college, they were there. When I was looking for counsel as I prepared to get married, they were there. As I went off to seminary and needed financial and prayer support, they were there. As my wife and I grieved the loss of our first child, they were there. They have been all a church body is supposed to be and more. I don't know where I'd be without their influence in my life. I can only hope and pray for the same for all of you.

Exercise: Talk with your leader about the following questions…What has been your experience of the church thus far in your life? What do you think the church is supposed to be and do? What kind of church do you think would be the best fit for your life and growth over the years to come? What churches in your community fit that description? How will you become involved in a church? When?

Nine: The Prayers

There may be nothing more important in growing an intimate relationship with God than prayer. But even as I say that I realize that our definition of prayer must be recognized, challenged, and modified. Prayer is so much more than just *talking at* God. It is being with God, listening to God, finding ourselves in the embrace of God, and so much more. Look at a few other definitions of prayer below:

Prayer is simply keeping company with God.
                              ~Clement of Alexadria

To pray is to descend with the mind into the heart, and there to stand before the face of the Lord, ever present, all-seeing within you.
                              ~St. Theophan

Prayer is the breath of the soul, the organ by which we receive Christ into our parched and withered hearts.
                              ~O. Hallesby

Prayer is creating a sacred space where you can be overwhelmed with God's uncompromising love and acceptance.
                              ~Michael Fonseca

True prayer is the divine in us appealing to the divine above us.
                              ~C. H. Dodd

Prayer is listening to the voice that calls you Beloved.
                              ~Henri J. M. Nouwen

All is prayer once it is perceived as such.
                              ~Robert Benson

Exercise: Which of these definitions are you most drawn to? Why? Write down your definition of prayer. Talk about it with your leader.

Read:
Matthew 6:5-15

What do these verses say about prayer? What do they say about how to pray? What wisdom do they give about what to pray?

Reflection:
I've always had a sneaking suspicion that there is much more to most things than meets the eye—prayer for instance. For years I was under the impression that prayer consisted of closing your eyes, bowing your head, and talking to God. The pictures and images of prayer that I carried around in my heart and mind, quite frankly, left much to be desired. Prayer was not an activity I was particularly drawn to or excited about. My guess is that this had much more to do with my definition of prayer than it did with the real practice of prayer. It wasn't until much later in life that I began to see that maybe my definition of prayer was far too small and rigid. Prayer wasn't so much about performing a duty as it was about building a wonderfully intimate relationship. Prayer was not simply throwing all the words I can muster at the unseen God, but it—at its very core—has always been about union with the God who lives within us. I think that's what Jesus is really getting at in Matthew 6; he is trying to recapture the true meaning and practice of prayer, which is simply being with God.

Don't stand on street corners, don't babble on and on; prayer is much more intimate and personal than that. Instead go into your closet—that space where true intimacy is possible—and shut the door. Leave everyone and everything else on the outside; I want it to be just me and you. I want us to be together in a way and a place where I have your undivided attention. I have so

much I want to say to you; so much of me that I want
you to know. And this space and time is the place where
that is most possible; the place where I can have the
deepest desires of my heart fulfilled, which is just to be
with you, my Beloved. Come inside where things are still
and quiet and you can hear every whisper of my loving
Spirit deep within your heart and soul. That's prayer.

"Here's what I want you to do: Find a quiet, secluded
place so you won't be tempted to role-play before God.
Just be there as simply and honestly as you can
manage. The focus will shift from you to God, and you
will begin to sense his grace." (Matthew 6:6 The
Message)

Question:
How will prayer become a regular part of your life with
God?

A final word:
Living life in Christ is about centering our lives
completely on Him. He is the hub of the wheel, around
which everything else revolves. Therefore, order your
minutes and your hours and your days around Him, not
vice versa. Relentlessly make space and time to be with
Him, to get to know Him. And as you spend more and
more time with Jesus I am convinced that you will fall
more and more in love with God. Allow that love (His
love for you and your love for Him) to determine
everything. May His love and peace be with you.

~Jim Branch
Summer 2005

Part Two
Forming Your Heart
(Establishing daily time with God)

A Word Before

Saint Augustine once said that the gospel of John is "a pool in which a child can wade or an elephant can swim." I have certainly found that to be true. For me it has been a place of great simplicity and a place of great mystery; a place to see God with my very own eyes and a place to ponder the depths and the complexities of His character. For years I have been drawn to John's account of the life of Jesus as a place of deep encounter and intimacy with God. Maybe that's because it's such a unique book of the Bible—so completely different from the other gospel accounts—containing stories and conversations that can be found nowhere else in scripture. Stories that seem more intent on showing us who Jesus is rather than simply what Jesus did. Stories that move a little slower than Mark and show us a little more of his interaction with people than Matthew. Stories that are told by one who saw himself as *"the disciple whom Jesus loved."* I long to see myself that way and my guess is that you long to see yourself that way as well—or you probably wouldn't be reading this book right now.

My hope in writing this part of the book is that you might encounter the love and care of the Father in its pages. That you might see something of the ebb and flow of God in my life as I have encountered Him and that it might somehow be helpful for your own journey. That I might be able to show you how God has used this gospel to form my heart and soul. It is my hope that God might seize your heart as well, that you might begin to get a sense of the intimacy that John had with Jesus and that Jesus longs to have with you. That Jesus might begin (or continue) to form your heart and soul. And most of all, that as you invest the next few days or weeks or months in this book you might encounter Jesus in a way that gives you the intimacy with God that you have only dreamt about or hoped for. God wants no less for you.

Hopefully the structure of this portion of the book will be nothing more than a little offering of space and time where you can be with Jesus. And as you spend more and more time with him you will be changed, you will begin to sense God's heart for you and be captured by his great affection. So use this book only as it is helpful—as a gentle guide. It is not a manual or a handbook, only a traveling companion. It is not meant to be a substitute for encounter with God but a space or structure to help you encounter Him. So whether you are child or elephant, God has a desire to speak with you through this gospel—so come on in, the water's fine.

Making This Part of the Book Work for You

As you go through this section of the book, it is my hope that you will learn how to be with God each day and that your time with him would have a certain "dance" to it that would help you find your way into His presence. I really believe the best way to do this is by exploration and repetition—finding a way that works well for you and repeating it over and over. For me (and for many others through the centuries) that dance has involves a daily rhythm of reading, reflection, response, and rest.

Start your time, therefore, with reading the text for the day. As you read, read slowly with a certain attentiveness to what the words are saying—or rather what God is saying to you through the words. As we have already seen, Hebrews 4:12 describes the Word of God as "living and active and sharper than any double edged sword." Believe that what you are reading is alive and that God is a God who longs to speak to you through it. He has something to say to you.

Also, as you read be attentive to certain words or images that might capture you for some reason. If you are drawn to a particular word or image, stop and reflect—begin to ask God what it is about that particular word or image that He wants you to see. If what you are reading is a gospel story, imagine yourself being one of the characters in the scene. What would you be feeling?

What would you be longing for? What would you need from Jesus at that moment? Ask yourself how that particular character is like you—and what does God want to say to you through that particular story? Read the text several times if need be—we are going for quality, not quantity. Allow the Word to work on you and move in you. In the words of Macrina Wiederkehr: "wear it like a robe."

After you have spent some time before God in reflection, spend some time responding to what God might be doing in you or saying to you. This response can take many forms. For instance, you might want to begin to record your thoughts and feelings in a journal each day. This would be a great way to monitor or track the movement of God in your life and heart. You might want to write your prayers to Him each day. Or write Him a poem or a song. You might want to draw a picture that expresses the appropriate response in some way. You might want to use some clay to mold or form something in response to the way God has spoken to you through the text. The questions listed each day may also help in this process. You must read them with an open heart and be honest in your responses for them to be fruitful.

Finally, rest. That's right, just rest in God's presence. Just be with God and allow him to comfort you with His embrace. Be attentive to Him. Listen to Him. After all, in reality, prayer is just being with God. In fact, Clement of Alexandria once said that prayer is simply "keeping company with God."

Hopefully this structure will offer you a good space for your soul to be formed by God. One of the most important parts of your relationship with Him is learning how to communicate with Him and how **He** communicates with you. Don't expect immediate success. It will take consistent work over a period of time—be patient with it—having your heart shaped by Him doesn't take place over night. Now, let's begin.

~Jim Branch (April 2004)

Day 1

Theme: Intimacy
Opening Prayer: O God, who existed before all things, draw near to my heart today as I draw near to yours. Grant that as we are together during this time, as well as this day, I will know of your presence to the core of my being. Let me experience the intimacy with you that I was created for. In the name of Jesus, the Word made flesh. Amen.

Read: John 1:1-2
In the beginning was the Word, and the Word was with God, and the Word was God. He was with God in the beginning.

Thoughts for Reflection:
The beginning of John's story has a familiar ring to it. In fact, his words are the very same words that begin all of the Scriptures (Genesis 1:1), "*In the beginning.*" Why in the world would John see fit to begin his account of the life of Jesus with these very same words? What is it that he is trying to help us see or understand?

Could it be that he wants us to know that even before the creation of the heavens and the earth there was already something (or better yet Someone) present—mysteriously and wonderfully present? Could it be that he wants us to know that before anything was made, God was there—Father, Son, and Spirit. One God, yet somehow three distinct persons (the Holy Trinity), connected by a love and an intimacy that we could not possibly understand; yet one we were created in the image of. It is a love and an intimacy we were made both to know and to reflect. God was so filled with love that He created us to be the objects of His great affection. As a great writer and poet of days gone by once said, "*We were created out of the laughter of the Trinity.*"

How in the world are we supposed to understand this? Well maybe the point is not so much to understand it, as to appreciate it. To appreciate that the very nature of our God is one of deep love and intimacy; an intimacy we were created to share in.

A second thing John seems to be trying to let his readers know is that Jesus is much bigger than we imagine—much larger than just the 33 years he lived on earth. Jesus (referred to as "the Word" in these verses) existed long before the creation of all things. In fact "*all things were created by him.*" In the beginning Jesus was already there, in some wonderfully unique relationship with God, and with the Spirit, in what some have called the *great round dance of love.*

You can see it in the very words John uses to describe this relationship. He says that before all things, Jesus was *with* God. The word *with* creates a picture of two people being face-to-face. Thus, Jesus was face-to-face with God (his Father) in a very beautiful and intimate way, as we, through Him, are invited to be. It's really amazing when you think about it; we are invited *into* this special relationship—this connectedness—through Jesus. So as you begin this new journey, please realize that this is one of God's chief desires for you; to know the nearness of your God.

For Your Journal: What does the word intimacy mean to you? Write about your desire for intimacy with God. Draw a picture, or write a poem if it is helpful.

For Prayer: Simply try to be with God for 5 minutes, no words, no requests, just sit in his presence and realize that He is with you. At the end of your time thank him for being near—because he was, whether you sensed him or not.

Day 2

Theme: You are created in His image
Opening Prayer: Almighty God, you created me in your image and called me to yourself, breathe your Divine Breath in me again today that I may remember who you are and who you made me to be. For the sake of Christ. Amen.

Read: John 1:3
Through him all things were made; without him nothing was made that has been made.

Thoughts for Reflection:
One of the biggest questions we all have in life is the question: "Who am I, really?" Most of life seems to be an attempt to provide ourselves, and our world, with the answer to that question. We try to answer it by what we look like, or by what we do, or by what we have—appearance, performance, or achievement. When we do this it is easy to believe that we have little, if any, value in the grand scheme of things. It is easy for us to forget that our value and our worth are not determined by any of these factors, but by the fact that we are created in the image of God.

Of all the things that God created, He created only us in His image. What better place to derive our worth than by the fact that the God of all creation "dreamt us into being." Before all things were created you were a thought in the mind of God (Ephesians 1:3-6 The Message); a thought that brought joy to his heart and a smile to his lips. In you God expressed himself in a unique and beautiful way that will never again be repeated. God formed you and made you "fearfully and wonderfully" (Psalm 139:14). He made you with great care and intention, to be a once-in-all-of-eternity expression of his character, grace and love. You are of incalculable value!

For Your Journal: Write yourself a letter from God telling you the things that delight him most about you.

Or write a letter to him thanking him for his care and design of the person he created you to be.

For Prayer: O Lord, my God, when I am tempted to look around and believe that I am worthless, remind me that I am the work of your hands and the delight of your heart; and that in your eyes I am priceless. Through Jesus. Amen.

.

Day 3

Theme: Life comes through finding your identity in Him.
Opening Prayer: O God, our heavenly Father, who created us beautifully and wonderfully, may we always look to you for our value and worth, remembering that we are a unique expression of your infinite love, care, and creativity. Help us, O Lord, to see ourselves as you see us—as objects of your extravagant love and tender affection. Through Christ. Amen.

Read: John 1:4-5
In him was life, and that life was the light of men. The light shines in the darkness, but the darkness has not understood it.

Thoughts for Reflection:
Our quest for life knows no bounds; we seek it with all of our time and energy. As a matter of fact if you look at how you spend your time it will give you a good idea of what you really believe will give you life—friends, things, romance, money, achievement, etc. But life, it seems, is a rather elusive creature. How do we get it? How do we keep it? What will really satisfy the deepest longings of my heart and soul?

In Him was life, John tells us. The fact of the matter is that real life comes only through Jesus. He is the only place that those created in His image are designed to find life. When we find our worth and value in Him and focus on relationship with Him; that is where we find true satisfaction, as we will later see in chapter 10. Do we really believe that Jesus can give us life? Do we really believe he wants to?

Author A. W. Tozer once said that the way we see God, in some ways, is the most important thing about us. I believe this is true. When I see God as the lover of my soul who desires to show me the life and the love I most deeply long for, both my life and my relationship with him are transformed. Do you see God as the giver of life? Or do you see him as the one who is trying to take it away? How you see him will make a huge difference in how you relate to him.

For Your Journal: Spend some time writing about where you seek life. Also, spend some time considering whether you see God as one who desires to give you life.

For Prayer: Give your deepest longings to God and receive from him the life he longs to give you at this very moment.

Day 4

Theme: God's voice, through John the Baptist.
Opening Prayer: Our Father, we thank you that you are a God who speaks, and we realize that you long for us to hear what you are saying to us in each moment of our lives. Speak to us in this time; that we may hear your voice and know the depths of your affection for us. In the name of Jesus, the True Light. Amen.

Read: John 1:6-9
There came a man who was sent from God; his name was John. He came as a witness to testify concerning that light, so that through him all men might believe. He himself was not the light; he came only as a witness to the light. The true light that gives life to every man was coming into the world.

Thoughts for Reflection:

For four hundred years (between the end of the Old Testament and the beginning of the New Testament) God was silent. From the last words of the prophet Malachi to the beginning of the gospels there was no prophetic voice of God among his people. Imagine what it would have been like for the people of God; wondering when—and if—God would ever speak to his people again. Generation after generation trying to follow him through the dark and silent world. Generation after generation trying to keep the faith even in the midst of despair and abandonment. Generation after generation totally forgetting what his voice even sounded like.

Then one day the Voice rings out in the wilderness— a voice that had a very unique quality to it. A voice that sounded familiar, but they couldn't quite place it. A voice that seemed to have some authority—some substance behind it. A voice that seemed to be filled with life and power. And so people went into the desert to listen to the Voice as it came out of the mouth of John the Baptist. Whether they came out of curiosity, or out of hope, or for entertainment—they came just the same. Many of them did not even know why they were so drawn to it.

God had broken his silence, in an unlikely place and through an unlikely looking person. And when He spoke, his voice was music to the ears (and hearts) of those who heard it; those who had been waiting, longing, and hoping. God had finally spoken again. He had spoken in order to prepare the way for how he would speak most directly and concretely to his lost world— through Jesus.

For Your Journal: Who in your life has been the voice of God to you? What did He say to you through them?

For Prayer: Look back on yesterday (or today if you are reading this at night) and try to remember all you did— paying attention to how, and where, and through whom God spoke to you (this is called the *Prayer of Examen*).

Listen for his voice in the events of your day. Listen for his voice right now. What is he saying to you?

Day 5

Theme: The Word made flesh
Opening Prayer: Almighty God, thank you that you are, ever and always, the God who comes. Thank you that you came to us in Jesus, and thank you that you still come to us today. Thank you that you just can't stay away, that your heart simply will not allow it. We thank you through Jesus, the Word made flesh. Amen.

Read: John 1:10-14
He was in the world, and though the world was made through him, the world did not recognize him. He came to that which was his own, but his own did not receive him. Yet to all who received him, to those who believed in his name, he gave the right to become children of God—children born not of natural descent, nor of human decision or a husband's will, but born of God. The Word became flesh and made his dwelling among us. We have seen his glory, the glory of the One and Only, who came from the Father, full of grace and truth.

Thoughts for Reflection:
    In the 1992 Summer Olympic Games in Barcelona there was a runner from Great Britain named Derrick Redmond. Redmond was a sprinter who had trained all of his life for this very moment in time—the time when he would represent his country in the 400 meters. It was the semifinal race and Redmond was ready for the challenge at hand. As the starter's gun went off, Redmond was out of the blocks quickly and on his way into the first turn. He was doing well, running hard, when in the middle of the back straightaway something snapped in the back of his right leg—it was his hamstring. As the other runners raced for the finish line

Derrick Redmond was left on the track in excruciating pain. After the race was finished, the race officials rushed to the aid of Derrick Redmond. Suddenly Redmond struggled to his feet and began to hop and limp his way around the track. In spite of the intense pain he was determined to finish the race. Seeing his struggle the fans began to rise and cheer him on in his efforts. As he was rounding the last turn a man appeared on the side of the track; he had come down out of the stands to help—it was Derrick Redmond's father Jim. Jim Redmond put his arm around his son and the two embraced as they walked slowly toward the finish line. Tears of pain and disappointment streamed down Derrick's face as the two finished the race to a standing ovation by the sellout crowd.

Jim Redmond just couldn't stay in the stands. As he saw his beloved child struggle on the track, his heart would not allow his feet to be still. Love had pulled him from the stands and down onto the track to wrap his arms around his son—to get involved in his pain. A father's heart is a beautiful thing to see.

That is what we see from these verses in John. We see a Father who just could not stand by and watch his beloved children struggle through this painful race of life. Love just would not allow his feet to be still. The Father came down out of the stands to wrap his arms around his creation, to get his hands involved in their struggle, to share their pain, and to show his deep affection for his children. God came to us. He wrapped himself in flesh and blood and became one of us—in the form of his Son, Jesus. He did this to show us the depths of his affection for us. The Word became flesh and made His dwelling among us.

Another Thought:

Before the beginning there was a Heart
And this Heart was the substance of God
It came from the very core of who God was
And was the very essence of God
      from before the beginning
Through his Heart God created all things

Without it nothing received the life-blood of God
This Heart was the source of true wholeness and peace
Its blood gave us the ability to see
To see the depths of the Heart
        in spite of all the darkness
Because the darkness is unable to stop its beating
And God ripped his Heart from his very chest
And he transplanted that Heart into one like us
Wrapping him in flesh and blood
And giving him a face and a name
And God's Heart lived among us
He walked with us and talked with us,
He laughed and cried with us
And we saw what God's Heart looked like
It was pumping with the blood of grace and truth
(a metaphorical representation of John 1:1-5, 14 JLB)

For Your Journal: Where in your week have you seen the Word made flesh? Where has God become most visible or real to you?

For Prayer: Thank God for the ways he has become flesh to you recently. Pray that he will allow you to be attentive to the ways he will become flesh to you today.

Day 6

Theme: Who is Jesus?

Opening Prayer: O God, our Father, thank you for the grace you have poured out upon us in your son Jesus. Help us to receive that grace again this day—that we might be reminded of your love and transformed into your likeness. Amen.

Read: John 1:15-18
John testifies concerning him. He cries out, saying, "This was he of whom I said, 'He who comes after me has surpassed me because he was before me.'" From the fullness of his grace we have all received one blessing after another. For the law was given through

Moses; grace and truth came through Jesus Christ. No one has ever seen God, but God the One and Only, who is at the Father's side, has made him known.

Thoughts for Reflection:

Someone once said that Jesus is the best photograph that God ever had taken of himself. Obviously, Jesus is much more than this, but it is a fitting description for this portion of John's writing. Jesus is the visible image of the invisible God (Colossians 1:15). He is God in the flesh. He is a picture of God for those who have never seen him before—which, as verse 18 points out, would include us all.

It is almost as if Jesus is God's portrait and John is the master painter. John's job is to fill in the details to show us what God is really like through painting a masterpiece of Jesus. As he begins his painting John tells us that a major color that must be used in painting this portrait is the color of grace. Grace at its core means unmerited favor. It is God's joyful gift of his love and affection to those who do not deserve it—us. You simply cannot paint a picture of God without it.

As John walks us through the next twenty chapters of his gospel, one of his main missions is to fill in the picture of God's grace through the interactions Jesus has with people just like us; to paint as many pictures of God as he can from as many different angles. As you look at these pictures—as you read and study these interactions—be attentive to what it shows you of the grace of God. In fact the gospel of John could easily be called "portraits of grace." So enjoy the tour and take a good long look at the grace of our God.

For Your Journal: Draw your own picture of God's grace.

For Prayer: Thank God for the places and the ways he has shown grace to you. Ask him to allow you to show grace to those in your world. Is there a particular person that God wants you to show grace to this day?

Day 7

Theme: Singing His song
Opening Prayer: Our Father, sing your song of love to us and through us this day—that your beauty and affection would be apparent to all who hear. In the name of Jesus, the Singer of the Song of Songs. Amen.

Read: John 1:19-28
Now this was John's testimony when the Jews of Jerusalem sent priests and Levites to ask him who he was. He did not fail to confess, but confessed freely, "I am not the Christ."

They asked him, "Then who are you? Are you Elijah?"

He said, "I am not."

"Are you the Prophet?"

He answered, "No."

Finally they said, "Who are you? Give us an answer to take back to those who sent us. What do you say about yourself?"

John replied in the words of Isaiah the prophet, "I am the voice of one calling in the desert, 'Make straight the way for the Lord.' "

Now some Pharisees who had been sent questioned him, "Why then do you baptize if you are not the Christ, nor Elijah, nor the Prophet?"

"I baptize with water," John replied, "but among you stands one you do not know. He is the one who comes after me, the thongs of whose sandals I am not worthy to untie."

This all happened at Bethany on the other side of the Jordan, where John was baptizing.

Thoughts for Reflection:
"Who are you?" That's the question constantly being asked of John the Baptist. "Are you somebody?" seems to be what the question implies. "Are you the Christ?"…"Are you a prophet?"…"Are you

important?"…"What is it about you that makes you special or valuable?"

"It's not who I am that makes me important?" John seems to say, "It's whose I am." John realizes that his value and worth are not measured by what people say or think about him—his value is determined by the One who made him, and called him, and put in him a song of hope for all people. It is the words and music of this song that gives his life purpose and direction and meaning.

John is God's messenger; given the privilege and responsibility of preparing the way for the Savior of the world. John is God's song; a beautiful and unique expression of God's goodness and beauty and creativity. He is a song that invites the hearers to know the affection of the Singer. John's job is to make sure the song gets sung…so he sings…and people are drawn to the desert by the beauty of the melody.

What about you? Did you know that you, like John the Baptist, are a wonderfully beautiful song of the God who made you to sing with passion to those that are walking in darkness? How will you let that song be sung in and through you today?

For Your Journal: Who are you? What is the song God has given you to sing?

For Prayer: Focus your prayers this day on gratitude for who God is and for who he made you to be. Ask him how he might desire you to sing his song today.

Day 8

Theme: What do you want?

Opening Prayer: Teach me to seek you, for I cannot seek you unless you teach me, or find you unless you show yourself to me. Let me seek you in my desire, and desire you in my seeking. Let me find you by loving you, let me love you when I find you.

~St. Anselm

Read: John 1:29-38

The next day John saw Jesus coming toward him and said, "Look, the Lamb of God, who takes away the sin of the world! This is the one I meant when I said, 'A man who comes after me has surpassed me because he was before me.' I myself did not know him, but the reason I came baptizing with water was that he might be revealed to Israel."

Then John gave this testimony: "I saw the Spirit come down from heaven as a dove and remain on him. I would not have known him, except that the one who sent me to baptize with water told me, 'The man on whom you see the Spirit come down and remain is he who will baptize with the Holy Spirit.' I have seen and I testify that this is the Son of God."

The next day John was there again with two of his disciples. When he saw Jesus passing by, he said, "Look, the Lamb of God!"

When the two disciples heard him say this, they followed Jesus. Turning around, Jesus saw them following and asked, "What do you want?"
They said, "Rabbi" (which means Teacher), "where are you staying?"

Thoughts for Reflection:

One of the things I want us to be especially attentive to as we journey through John's gospel together are the questions that Jesus asks. Any time we see a question mark following the words of Christ, I want us to stop and consider it. As we do this I believe we will find that these questions are not only significant to the people he asked them to, but to us as well. They are questions that seem to cut right to the heart of the major issues of life and faith.

In this instance the question he asks these two brand new disciples is: "What do you want?" Or, more literally, "What do you seek?" What an incredibly profound and appropriate question to ask these men—after all, they have just decided to leave John the Baptist and turn and follow Jesus. Why? What are they looking for? What are they hoping to find? What are they seeking? What do they really want?

What about you? If Jesus were to ask you this question what would your answer be? What do you really want?

For Your Journal: What do you want?

For Prayer: Spend your prayer time today putting the deepest longings of your heart before God. Ask him to increase your longing for him.

Day 9

Theme: Come and See

Opening Prayer: Lord Jesus, thank you for your invitation to "come and see." Help me to take you up on that invitation during this time, as well as the rest of this day. In your name. Amen.

Read: John 1:39
"Come," he replied, "and you will see."
So they went and saw where he was staying, and spent that day with him. It was about the tenth hour.

Thoughts for Reflection:
Come. It is Jesus' word to the first disciples—and also his word to all those disciples who would come after them. As a matter of fact it is his word to you this day— an invitation. It is a word that he uttered often; and still utters constantly to all who will hear. It is an open invitation to be with him in the ebb and flow of this day.

All of life holds this invitation—every moment, every situation, every circumstance, every event. All that is required of us is to be attentive to its utterance and open to its leading. The most ordinary situation you encounter today can hold the call to "*come*" if we have the ears to hear. This will be one of the most important elements of

your spiritual journey throughout the course of your life—
so begin now to listen well for that word of life... *Come.*
For Your Journal: Have there been times in your life
when you have heard God's invitation to come? How do
you think God is inviting you to come today? What will
that mean?
For Prayer: Ask God what his invitation is for you today.
Thank him for the ways he has called you to *come* in the
past.

Day 10

Theme: A new name
Opening Prayer: Heavenly Father, thank you that
before you created all things you knew my name—not
just the name my parents gave me, but the name you
picked out especially for me—a perfect expression of
who you made me to be. Thank you that when you say
that name it brings joy to your heart and a smile to your
lips; as well as to mine. Help me to bear it well. In the
name of Jesus—the Name above all Names. Amen

Read: John 1:40-42
*Andrew, Simon Peter's brother, was one of the two who
heard what John had said and who had followed Jesus.
The first thing Andrew did was to find his brother Simon
and tell him, "We have found the Messiah" (that is, the
Christ). And he brought him to Jesus.*

*Jesus looked at him and said, "You are Simon son of
John. You will be called Cephas" (which, when
translated, is Peter).*

Thoughts for Reflection:
In most cultures naming something gives it value—
this is especially true in the life of Israel. Throughout the
Old Testament whenever a person or place was named
it was done with great care and intention, as if its name
would somehow reflect the true character of the person

or significance of the event. And often someone's name was changed by God to be a better expression of who they were becoming: Abram (exalted father) becomes Abraham (father of multitudes), Jacob (deceiver) becomes Israel (struggles with God), Saul (asked for) becomes Paul (small), and Simon becomes Peter (rock).

It is as if God has pet names for his children that are a perfect expression of who they were made to be. Revelation 2:17 tells us that when the new heaven and new earth arrive, God will also give us a new name. It will be a name that was picked out especially for us—and will be written on a white stone. In Simon's case it was almost as if Jesus couldn't wait to tell him his special name—Cephas (also translated Peter, which means Rock).

God has a special name for you too. It is a name that when he utters it will resonate deeply within you because it will be a perfect description of who you really are at your core.

For Your Journal: Where did your name come from? Do you like it? Does it make you feel special? What nicknames do people use for you? Do they bring you joy or pain? Are they really expressions of who you are? How do you feel when people call you that? What do you think God's special name for you is? What do you long for it to be?

For Prayer: Spend your prayer time today listening to the Voice that calls you Beloved.

Day 11

Theme: Follow me

Opening Prayer: Lord Jesus, thank you that, like Philip, you came and *found* me—even when I wasn't particularly looking for you. And thank you that when you found me, you invited me to follow you; which demands that I leave my old life and my old ways behind and begin life anew—with you. Be my guide for this new adventure and my companion along the way. Be my friend and be my Savior. Be my Lord and be my all. In the name of Jesus. Amen.

Read: John 1:43-51

The next day Jesus decided to leave for Galilee. Finding Philip, he said to him, "Follow me." Philip, like Andrew and Peter, was from the town of Bethsaida. Philip found Nathanael and told him, "We have found the one Moses wrote about in the Law, and about whom the prophets also wrote--Jesus of Nazareth, the son of Joseph."

"Nazareth! Can anything good come from there?" Nathanael asked.

"Come and see," said Philip.

When Jesus saw Nathanael approaching, he said of him, "Here is a true Israelite, in whom there is nothing false."

"How do you know me?" Nathanael asked.

Jesus answered, "I saw you while you were still under the fig tree before Philip called you."

Then Nathanael declared, "Rabbi, you are the Son of God; you are the King of Israel."

Jesus said, "You believe because I told you I saw you under the fig tree. You shall see greater things than that." He then added, "I tell you the truth, you shall see heaven open, and the angels of God ascending and descending on the Son of Man."

Thoughts for Reflection:

Nathaniel was a reflective guy. He thought a lot about everything, especially about God. He studied the Scriptures constantly, waiting and watching and longing for the day the Messiah would come to save Israel.

On this particular day he was sitting under a fig tree, his usual place for reading and prayer and reflection. And he was most likely reading about how God came to Jacob in a vision and showed him a ladder reaching up to heaven on which the very angels of the Lord were ascending and descending from heaven to earth.

As he was reading, his brother Philip came running up to him, excitedly telling him about the One they had found—or rather the One who had found them. *The One Moses had written about in the Law, and about whom the prophets also wrote.* His name was Jesus, the son of Joseph, and he was from Nazareth.

Nathaniel was skeptical...Nazareth? Surely the Messiah would never come from Nazareth; it was a small, insignificant, obscure little place that was never even mentioned in the Old Testament. Would the Messiah of the Most High God really come from a lowly, invisible place like that? But in spite of his skepticism, he goes along with Philip to meet this "Messiah."

And when he first sees Jesus, he is met by words that totally catch him off guard, *"Here is a true Israelite, in whom there is nothing false."* It was almost Jesus looked right into him and told him what he saw, for indeed Nathaniel's heritage and religion were of utmost importance to him. *"How do you know me?"* he utters in surprise and amazement.

And if what he had already said wasn't enough, what Jesus says next really blows him away. *"I saw you while you were still under the fig tree before Philip called you."* Jesus replies, with a bit of an amused smile beginning to form on his lips. And that's enough for Nathaniel, he's sold, he believes, he's in, *"Rabbi, you are the Son of God; you are the King of Israel."*

But Jesus is not done, he goes on, *"I tell you the truth, you shall see heaven open, and the angels of God ascending and descending on the Son of Man."* Not only had Jesus seen Nathaniel under the tree, but He even knew the very Scripture he was reading while he was sitting there.

So Philip and Nathaniel—like Peter and Andrew, and James and John right before them—decide to leave everything behind and follow Him. They leave their homes and their towns, they leave their jobs and their possessions, they leave their families and their friends. They leave behind all that is familiar in order to follow the One who Moses wrote about in the Law, the One who knew them better and loved them deeper than anyone or anything ever could. They had been found by the Messiah and from this day on nothing would ever be the same.

For Your Journal: What does it mean for you to follow Jesus? Where is He leading you right now? What does He want most from you? What might you need to leave behind?

For Prayer: Pray about the ways God might desire for you to follow him. Listen for His leading in your life. Ask Him for the courage necessary to go wherever He leads.

Day 12

Theme: A Surprising God

Opening Prayer: O God of life, thank you that you are the creator of fullness, and joy, and celebration. Fill me this day with the richness of your kingdom. In the name of Jesus, who turns water into wine. Amen.

Read: John 2:1-11

On the third day a wedding took place at Cana in Galilee. Jesus' mother was there, and Jesus and his disciples had also been invited to the wedding. When the wine was gone, Jesus' mother said to him, "They have no more wine."

"Dear woman, why do you involve me?" Jesus replied, "My time has not yet come."

His mother said to the servants, "Do whatever he tells you."

Nearby stood six stone water jars, the kind used by the Jews for ceremonial washing, each holding from twenty to thirty gallons. Jesus said to the servants, "Fill the jars with water"; so they filled them to the brim.

Then he told them, "Now draw some out and take it to the master of the banquet." They did so, and the master of the banquet tasted the water that had been turned into wine. He did not realize where it had come from, though the servants who had drawn the water knew. Then he called the bridegroom aside and said, "Everyone brings out the choice wine first and then the cheaper wine after the guests have had too much to drink; but you have saved the best till now."

This, the first of his miraculous signs, Jesus performed in Cana of Galilee. He thus revealed his glory, and his disciples put their faith in him.

Thoughts for Reflection:

In the Jewish culture a wedding was a time of great celebration—usually taking place over a three or four-day period— involving food and friends, family and fun, wine and music, dancing and rejoicing. Exactly the kind of place you would expect God to show up, right? Just the setting you would imagine for his first miracle to be performed? Probably not.

How many of us would have written this script? Jesus' first miracle—turning water into wine at a three-day party. Most of us might have expected him to do the exact opposite—turn the wine into water, but he doesn't. What a surprise! Maybe God is different than what we might think. Maybe he is a God that enjoys celebration and laughter and life. Maybe his real concern is the quality of our lives. Why else would he have taken water jars that were used by the Jews to heap more and more rules on the average worshiper and turn them into vessels of the richest, fullest, best wine available?

Why would He have chosen this to be His first miracle? Maybe just to show people that he was not at all what they expected. Maybe just to show people that he is more interested in relationships than rules, in giving life than taking it away, in fullness than emptiness; he is intimately concerned with the quality of our lives. Maybe his deepest desire is to turn the ordinary water of our lives into the rich, full, wine of the Kingdom.

For Your Journal: What is your picture of Jesus? How does this story surprise you? How might the real Jesus be different from what you have thought?

For Prayer: Ask God to show you who he really is.

Day 13

Theme: God's response to sin
Opening Prayer: Search me O God and know me. Test me and know my anxious thoughts. See if there is any offensive way in me and lead me in the way everlasting. (Psalm 139:23-24)

Read: John 2:12-17
After this he went down to Capernaum with his mother and brothers and his disciples. There they stayed for a few days. When it was almost time for the Jewish Passover, Jesus went up to Jerusalem. In the temple courts he found men selling cattle, sheep and doves, and others sitting at tables exchanging money. So he made a whip out of cords, and drove all from the temple area, both sheep and cattle; he scattered the coins of the money changers and overturned their tables. To those who sold doves he said, "Get these out of here! How dare you turn my Father's house into a market!"

His disciples remembered that it is written: "Zeal for your house will consume me."

Thoughts For Reflection:
The religious leaders of Jesus' day were a creative bunch. They were experts at figuring out how to exploit the people in the name of worship. On this occasion they had a pretty elaborate scam going on to take advantage of the people—especially the poor. They first set up inspection stations to make sure the sacrifices that were brought by the people to be used in worship were acceptable—of course most of them were not. After each person was told their animal was not an acceptable sacrifice, they set up booths to sell them a new sheep, dove, etc. to sacrifice—possibly the very animals others had brought to sacrifice that were deemed unacceptable.

Also, in order to buy these animals they had to use "temple money" which meant their money had to be converted at a huge loss to the worshipper. All in all it was a very expensive venture—especially for the poor. Inevitably the only sacrifice the poor man could afford was a dove.

This was the scene Jesus walked into on this particular day. No wonder he was so angry. The very ones that were supposed to be caring for the spiritual needs of the people were the ones taking advantage of them. As a matter of fact it angered Jesus so much that he began turning over the tables and driving out the sellers with a whip. His heart could not bear to see what was going on, so He intervened on their behalf.

The bottom line is: sin angers God. As we see throughout the entire bible, God takes sin very seriously. He will not tolerate it. He will overturn the tables of those that have it in their hearts. Wherever there is sin, there is God's anger (or wrath as it is called in the Old Testament). God takes sin so seriously that he requires it to be paid for in full. Thus Jesus comes to earth to die for sinners—to satisfy God's anger over our sin, for those that trust Him with their lives.

For Your Journal: What does this scene tell us about God's response to sin? Are there tables in your life that need to be turned over by God? Moneychangers that need to be driven out? What are they?

For Prayer: Spend your time in prayer this morning in confession, telling God all of the things and /or places you need his mercy and forgiveness. Then ask him to drive those things out of the temple of your heart.

Day 14

Theme: Demanding a sign.

Opening Prayer: Lord Jesus, help me to come to you in spirit and in truth this day—that I might come on your terms and not my own. Help my eyes to be open to the ways you will entrust yourself to me today. In your mighty name, Amen.

Read: John 2:18-25

Then the Jews demanded of him, "What miraculous sign can you show us to prove your authority to do all this?" Jesus answered them, "Destroy this temple, and I will raise it again in three days." The Jews replied, "It has taken forty-six years to build this temple, and you are going to raise it in three days?" But the temple he had spoken of was his body. After he was raised from the dead, his disciples recalled what he had said. Then they believed the Scripture and the words that Jesus had spoken. Now while he was in Jerusalem at the Passover Feast, many people saw the miraculous signs he was doing and believed in his name. But Jesus would not entrust himself to them, for he knew all men. He did not need man's testimony about man, for he knew what was in a man.

Thoughts for Reflection:

The Jews demanded a sign. Can you imagine that? Demanding a sign from the God of the universe? Challenging God Almighty to prove Himself. Trying to use the King of Kings to serve our own purposes? They wanted Jesus to behave according to their wishes, their desires, and their expectations, or they would not even acknowledge him. He had to jump through their hoops to be their God. They were only interested in a God they could control, because control was a really big deal for them—as it is for us.

Jesus, therefore, decides not to *entrust* himself to them. He gives all kinds of signs to the average seeker, but none to those that demand it. Why? What is the lesson here? Is it that Jesus only comes to us on his terms, not our own? That even though he comes to us on our *turf*, he only comes on his *terms*. He is the one in control and he will not give it up. You can't demand that God behave the way you want or he won't show up at all. When we try and dictate how and when God will come to us, we stop seeking him altogether and start seeking our own agenda. Thus we are no longer seeking God at all; we are seeking to become God.

For Your Journal: Do you ever demand things of God? What demands are you making of him right now in your life? What does that lead to? How does it make you feel? What do you think God's response is to your demandingness?

For Prayer: Ask God to come to you on His terms today. Ask him to tell you what he wants to do in your life. Listen for his answer and write down what you hear him say.

Day 15

Theme: Born again.

Opening Prayer: O Loving God, who breathed me into being, breathe your Divine Breath in me again this day; that I might be filled with your life and guided by the winds of your Spirit. For the sake of your Son. Amen.

Read: John 3:1-15

Now there was a man of the Pharisees named Nicodemus, a member of the Jewish ruling council. He came to Jesus at night and said, "Rabbi, we know you are a teacher who has come from God. For no one could perform the miraculous signs you are doing if God were not with him."

In reply Jesus declared, "I tell you the truth, no one can see the kingdom of God unless he is born again."

"How can a man be born when he is old?" Nicodemus asked. "Surely he cannot enter a second time into his mother's womb to be born!"

Jesus answered, "I tell you the truth, no one can enter the kingdom of God unless he is born of water and the Spirit. Flesh gives birth to flesh, but the Spirit gives birth to spirit. You should not be surprised at my saying, 'You must be born again.' The wind blows wherever it pleases. You hear its sound, but you cannot tell where it comes from or where it is going. So it is with everyone born of the Spirit."

"How can this be?" Nicodemus asked.

"You are Israel's teacher," said Jesus, "and do you not understand these things? I tell you the truth, we speak of what we know, and we testify to what we have seen, but still you people do not accept our testimony. I have spoken to you of earthly things and you do not believe; how then will you believe if I speak of heavenly things? No one has ever gone into heaven except the one who came from heaven—the Son of Man. Just as Moses lifted up the snake in the desert, so the Son of Man must be lifted up, that everyone who believes in him may have eternal life.

Thoughts for Reflection:

New birth is an essential part of the spiritual life. Nicodemus is racking his brain trying to understand something in physical terms that can only be understood spiritually. And anyone who has experienced the **grace** of being *born again*—or born from above, or born of the Spirit—knows exactly what Jesus is talking about.

It is not something you can explain, or control, or manipulate. It is rather something that happens to you, much the same way being born *happens* to a baby. He or she has absolutely no control over the process, that is totally up to Someone much bigger than they. They have no control over their conception, or pregnancy, or birth; all they can do is *be born*. This is the mystery that Jesus is trying to explain to Nicodemus...and us as well.

When we trust Jesus with our lives, it is solely because He has been at work—by His Spirit—deep within us, bringing something into being that was not there before. His Spirit, in a sense, is born within us and we, therefore, become new creations. And after we *become* (literally *come to be*) we then begin to try and figure out—in cooperation with His Spirit—how to nurture and grow this life of God within us.

For Your Journal: Draw a picture that describes this new life that was born in you.

For Prayer: Thank God for this new birth and ask him to show you how to nurture and grow this new life in the days and weeks ahead.

Day 16

Theme: God's love

Opening Prayer: I feel your love as you hold me to your sacred heart, my beloved Jesus, my God, my Master, but I feel, too, the need I have of your tenderness, and your caress because of my infinite weakness.

~Charles De Foucauld

Read: John 3:16

For God so loved the world that he gave his one and only Son, that whoever believes in him shall not perish but have eternal life.

Thoughts for Reflection: More than anything else the life of faith is a life of love—God's incredible love for us and our love (in response) for him. It is the knowledge of his love that will change everything. A knowledge of the heart rather than just the head. When we begin to understand the extravagance of God's love, our hearts are completely captured by love for him in return. When we taste his great affection, it will completely reorder our affections.

Here (John 3:16) Jesus gives us a brief glimpse at this amazing love. A love so great that He gave his son for us—that we might spend eternity with the Lover of our souls. Nothing else in all of Scripture is more important to understand than this. If we can begin to grasp the height and depth and breadth of His love everything else will fall into place.

Do you know how deeply you are loved by the God who made you? His love for you is beyond limits. His love for you is without measure. His love for you cannot be overstated. His love for you is total and complete. His love for you will never fail.

More Thoughts: Nothing is more practical than finding God, than falling in love [with Him] in a quite absolute, final way. What you are in love with, what seizes your imagination, will affect everything.

It will decide what will get you out of bed in the morning, what you will do with your evening, how you spend your weekends, what you read, whom you know, what breaks your heart, and what amazes you with joy and gratitude. Fall in love, stay in love, and it will decide everything.

~Fr. Pedro Arrupe

For Your Journal: Do you really believe God loves you deeply and passionately? Why or why not? Write yourself a love letter from God.

For Prayer: Spend your time in prayer today imagining yourself in the embrace of God. Listen to him tell you how deeply He loves you.

Day 17

Theme: Saved

Opening Prayer: Thank you Lord Jesus that you came to earth to save sinners, to rescue us from eternal death. Help us to fully understand the implications of this rescue, that we may love you with all of our hearts and souls and minds and strength. Through Christ. Amen.

Read: John 3:17-21

For God did not send his Son into the world to condemn the world, but to save the world through him. Whoever believes in him is not condemned, but whoever does not believe stands condemned already because he has not believed in the name of God's one and only Son. This is the verdict: Light has come into the world, but men loved darkness instead of light because their deeds were evil. Everyone who does evil hates the light, and

*will not come into the light for fear that his deeds will be
exposed. But whoever lives by the truth comes into the
light, so that it may be seen plainly that what he has
done has been done through God.*

Thoughts for Reflection: *Saved.* It's a word we hear
often in religious circles. So often, in fact, that it could
have begun to lose its meaning. John tells us that Jesus
didn't come into the world to condemn it, but to *save* it.
What does that mean? Why do we need to be *saved*?
And what do we need to be *saved* from?

From the beginning we were created by God to love
him and to be in relationship with him—to find our life
and value and meaning in him. Very early on in the
story, however (Genesis 3), we decide we would rather
find life and love and meaning in other places, so we
turn from God and set out on our own. This choice to
set out on our own rather than follow God is the
definition of the word *sin*. As a result of this choice we
are cut off from our source of life; and God was very
clear from the beginning that if we cut ourselves off from
our source of life the result would be death. Therefore,
because of sin we all experience death—separation from
the God who made us for life.

As a matter of fact Ephesians 2:1-8 tells us that
because of sin, we not only will experience eternal
death, but we are already spiritually dead now because
of our separation from God. This news is not terribly
hard to believe because most of us, in our heart of
hearts, know that something is terribly wrong on the
inside. But the passage also tells us that while we were
dead, God (because of his extravagant love) decided to
intervene on our behalf—to save us, to rescue us, to
make us alive again through the death of Jesus on the
cross. So God takes action to save us *from* eternal
death and separation.

But he doesn't just save us *from* something he also
saves us *for* something, He saves us *for* himself, *for*
life—full, rich life focused on his unfailing love. God's
desire is not that we spend our entire lives trying to keep

from going to hell, but that we spend life enjoying the richness of his love and affection and sharing that with those who are still "walking in darkness."

More Thoughts: On January 13, 1982 an Air Florida plane that had just taken off from Washington National Airport crashed into the northbound span of the 14th Street Bridge and plunged into the icy Potomac River less than one mile from the airport. Of the 79 passengers on board, only six of them survived the initial crash—one of whom sacrificed his life for the lives of his fellow passengers as they struggled to stay alive in the icy water by hanging on to the twisted wreckage. His name was Arland D. Williams. Here's how one witness reported the heroic feat:

> "He was about 50 years old, one of half a dozen survivors clinging to twisted wreckage bobbing in the icy Potomac when the first helicopter arrived. To the copter's two-man Park Police crew he seemed the most alert. Life vests were dropped, then a flotation ball. The man passed them to the others. On two occasions, the crew recalled, he handed away a life line from the hovering machine that could have dragged him to safety. The helicopter crew - who rescued five people, the only persons who survived from the jetliner - lifted a woman to the riverbank, then dragged three more persons across the ice to safety. Then the life line saved a woman who was trying to swim away from the sinking wreckage, and the helicopter pilot, Donald W. Usher, returned to the scene, but the man was gone," from "A Hero - Passenger Aids Others, Then Dies", **The Washington Post**, January 14, 1982.

Arland D. Williams was a hero—giving up his life for the lives of others in need of rescue.

For many years since the time of this heroic feat it has been used to explain the great lengths God has gone to in order to rescue us—giving up his own Son in order to save us from eternal death. The explanation revolves around the idea that as we were struggling in the icy waters of sin, in need of a savior, then God lowered a life line to us through Christ, who died that we may live. Our job is to grab hold of the life line in order to assure our rescue.

This story, however (as great as it is), doesn't seem go far enough in telling the full extent of what God really did in rescuing us from sin. As we've seen already, Ephesians 2:1-8 tells us that we weren't just struggling in the icy waters of sin—we were completely dead. We were on the bottom of the Potomac with no breath and no pulse (in our spirit). There was not one thing we could do to save ourselves. We couldn't even grab a life line—we were dead. So God did it all—He dove into the icy waters, pulled our (spiritually) lifeless bodies off the bottom of the river, brought us to the surface, and breathed the breath of life back into our dead souls. It was all Him. *He made us alive through Christ.* Now that is a rescue! Now that is something to be grateful for!

For Your Journal: What does it mean to you that God has saved you? Write a letter to express your gratitude to Him.

For Prayer: Remember the day of your rescue. Relive it. Thank Him for your salvation and the people and experiences he used to breathe life into your lifeless spirit.

Day 18

Theme: Receive, listen, wait
Opening Prayer: Lord, teach me to listen.

Read: John 3:22-30

After this, Jesus and his disciples went out into the Judean countryside, where he spent some time with them, and baptized. Now John also was baptizing at Aenon near Salim, because there was plenty of water, and people were constantly coming to be baptized. (This was before John was put in prison.) An argument developed between some of John's disciples and a certain Jew over the matter of ceremonial washing. They came to John and said to him, "Rabbi, that man who was with you on the other side of the Jordan—the one you testified about—well, he is baptizing, and everyone is going to him."

To this John replied, "A man can receive only what is given him from heaven. You yourselves can testify that I said, 'I am not the Christ but am sent ahead of him.' The bride belongs to the bridegroom. The friend who attends the bridegroom waits and listens for him, and is full of joy when he hears the bridegroom's voice. That joy is mine, and it is now complete. He must become greater; I must become less.

Thoughts for Reflection: One of the truths of the kingdom is that life with God cannot be seized, or manipulated, or controlled—as much as we would like to believe that it can be. As we can see in these words of Jesus, life with God is much more about receiving, and listening, and waiting than it is about doing. When we realize this and begin to put it into practice, only then will we be able to experience the intimacy that God longs for with us—intimacy that will form our hearts and change our lives. In fact, the measure of our spiritual progress might have more to do with becoming more receptive (and listening for his voice) than anything else.

When we wait on the Lord, and listen for His voice, and receive what he has to tell us, then our hearts are transformed into his likeness. We become more and more like the God we love. Then *He begins to increase* and *we begin to decrease.* Our intimacy with him and our love for him guide our thoughts and actions.

Therefore, the cultivation of our attentiveness and receptivity might be a couple of the most important aspects of our life with God. How do we cultivate an attitude of receptivity? How do we attune our ears to His voice? What does it mean to wait on Him?

For Your Journal: What does it mean for you to be receptive to God? What do you sense God wants you to receive from him? How will you listen to God? What do you think he wants to tell you?

For Prayer: Spend ten minutes just listening to God. After you are done pick up your journal and write about the experience. What was it like? What was difficult? What do you sense God was trying to say to you? Try this discipline daily at the end of your time with him.

Day 19

Theme: The One from above

Opening Prayer: O Heavenly Father, thank you that you are above all; that your thoughts are higher than our thoughts and your ways higher than our ways. Thank you also that you sent Jesus to show us the way to heaven; that we might be with you for all eternity. We pray in the name of Jesus, the Eternal Son. Amen.

Read: John 3:31-36

"The one who comes from above is above all; the one who is from the earth belongs to the earth, and speaks as one from the earth. The one who comes from heaven is above all. He testifies to what he has seen and heard, but no one accepts his testimony. The man who has accepted it has certified that God is truthful. For the one whom God has sent speaks the words of God, for God gives the Spirit without limit. The Father loves the Son and has placed everything in his hands. Whoever believes in the Son has eternal life, but

whoever rejects the Son will not see life, for God's wrath remains on him."

Thoughts for Reflection: John began his gospel with the God *above* coming down to earth and dwelling *among* us. What incredible news! God above has come down to be one of us. The Creator of all that is becomes part of His creation—giving flesh to God—so that we could see him, and know him, and be saved by him.

It is easy as we hear this incredible story to forget that this same Jesus is also God (in the flesh). He is not a superhero, or a prophet, or a religious leader, or just a great teacher—but God in the flesh. And though he could be seen, he can never be totally comprehended.

John reminds us of that here, continuously stating that Jesus is *from above*. That He is the one who created all things (John 1:3). As a matter of fact Colossians 1:15-16 tells us that, "He is the image of the invisible God"…and that…"all things were created by him and for him." Lest we get too comfortable with Jesus, we must remember that it was He that:

> *measured the waters in the hollow of his hand, and with the breadth of his hand marked off the heavens.* He that *has held the dust of the earth in a basket, and weighed the mountains on the scales and the hills in a balance.* (Isaiah 40:12)

And it is He that:

> *brings out the starry host one by one, and calls them each by name.* (Isaiah 40:26)

I have a friend that teaches astrophysics at a prominent university in the south. He was telling me one day of the vastness of the universe—just in sheer numbers of stars. He said that on any clear night you could possibly see 3,000 stars with the naked eye. There are, however, around 10^{21} stars in our galaxy alone—that's 1,000,000,000,000,000,000,000. And to take it a step further, there are an estimated 70 billion galaxies. And Jesus is the one that put them all in place and calls them out each night by name. The same Jesus that came to earth so that through him we might have eternal life...through the One who is *from above*.

So we must recognize that even when we try to fathom the immensity of creation, we must always keep in mind that He is bigger still. He is more vast than all the waters of earth, larger than the highest mountains, more endless that the heavens. He is truly *from above*. When we start getting too comfortable with the Jesus we know, we must remember that we are only beginning to scratch the surface of who he really is—which makes the incarnation so much more amazing. The God who calls the stars by name, also knows my name, and somehow became a baby in a manger! Incredible!

More Thoughts:

The *heavens praise your wonders, O Lord, your faithfulness too, in the assembly of the holy ones. For who in the skies above can compare with the Lord? Who is like you among the heavenly beings. In the council of the holy ones God is greatly feared; he is more awesome than all who surround him. O Lord God Almighty, who is like you? You are mighty, O Lord, and your faithfulness surrounds you. You rule over the surging sea; when its waves mount up you still them...*

The heavens are yours, and yours also the earth; you founded the world and all that is in it. You created the north and the south; Tabor and Hermon sing for joy at your name. Your arm is endued with power; your hand is strong, your right hand exalted.

Psalm 89:5-13

For Your Journal: What does it mean to you that Jesus is *from above*? What does it add to your picture of Jesus? To your understanding of God? What do you think God wants to tell you through these verses? Draw a picture of God's greatness or write about a time when you remember thinking "Wow" about his power.

For Prayer: Spend at least ten minutes contemplating God's greatness. Then spend the next ten thanking him for it.

Day 20

Theme: Thirst

Opening Prayer: You called, You cried, you shattered my deafness. You sparkled, you blazed, You drove away my blindness. You shed your fragrance, and I drew in my breath, and I pant for You. I tasted and now I hunger and thirst. You touched me, and now I burn with longing for your peace.

~St. Augustine

Read: John 4:1-42

The Pharisees heard that Jesus was gaining and baptizing more disciples than John, although in fact it was not Jesus who baptized, but his disciples. When the Lord learned of this, he left Judea and went back once more to Galilee.

Now he had to go through Samaria. So he came to a town in Samaria called Sychar, near the plot of ground Jacob had given to his son Joseph. Jacob's well was there, and Jesus, tired as he was from the journey, sat down by the well. It was about the sixth hour.

When a Samaritan woman came to draw water, Jesus said to her, "Will you give me a drink?" (His disciples had gone into the town to buy food.)

The Samaritan woman said to him, "You are a Jew and I am a Samaritan woman. How can you ask me for a drink?" (For Jews do not associate with Samaritans)

Jesus answered her, "If you knew the gift of God and who it is that asks you for a drink, you would have asked him and he would have given you living water."

"Sir," the woman said, "you have nothing to draw with

and the well is deep. Where can you get this living water? Are you greater than our father Jacob, who gave us the well and drank from it himself, as did also his sons and his flocks and herds?"

Jesus answered, "Everyone who drinks this water will be thirsty again, but whoever drinks the water I give him will never thirst. Indeed, the water I give him will become in him a spring of water welling up to eternal life."

The woman said to him, "Sir, give me this water so that I won't get thirsty and have to keep coming here to draw water."

He told her, "Go, call your husband and come back."

"I have no husband," she replied.

Jesus said to her, "You are right when you say you have no husband. The fact is, you have had five husbands, and the man you now have is not your husband. What you have just said is quite true."

"Sir," the woman said, "I can see that you are a prophet. Our fathers worshiped on this mountain, but you Jews claim that the place where we must worship is in Jerusalem."

Jesus declared, "Believe me, woman, a time is coming when you will worship the Father neither on this mountain nor in Jerusalem. You Samaritans worship what you do not know; we worship what we do know, for salvation is from the Jews. Yet a time is coming and has now come when the true worshipers will worship the Father in spirit and truth, for they are the kind of worshipers the Father seeks. God is spirit, and his worshipers must worship in spirit and in truth."

The woman said, "I know that Messiah" (called Christ) "is coming. When he comes, he will explain everything to us."

Then Jesus declared, "I who speak to you am he."

Just then his disciples returned and were surprised to find him talking with a woman. But no one asked, "What do you want?" or "Why are you talking with her?"

Then, leaving her water jar, the woman went back to the town and said to the people, "Come, see a man who told me everything I ever did. Could this be the Christ?"

They came out of the town and made their way toward him.

Meanwhile his disciples urged him, "Rabbi, eat something."

But he said to them, "I have food to eat that you know nothing about."

Then his disciples said to each other, "Could someone have brought him food?"

"My food," said Jesus, "is to do the will of him who sent me and to finish his work. Do you not say, 'Four months more and then the harvest'? I tell you, open your eyes and look at the fields! They are ripe for harvest. Even now the reaper draws his wages, even now he harvests the crop for eternal life, so that the sower and the reaper may be glad together. Thus the saying 'One sows and another reaps' is true. I sent you to reap what you have not worked for. Others have done the hard work, and you have reaped the benefits of their labor."

Many of the Samaritans from that town believed in him because of the woman's testimony, "He told me everything I ever did."

So when the Samaritans came to him, they urged him to stay with them, and he stayed two days. And because of his words many more became believers.

They said to the woman, "We no longer believe just because of what you said; now we have heard for ourselves, and we know that this man really is the Savior of the world."

Thoughts for Reflection: Jesus is interested in the quality of our lives. If you don't believe it, just take a good long look at this story. It is the story of a lonely woman, desperate for love; so much so that she has had five husbands, going on six, and none of them have been able to give her the love and the fullness she is desperately longing for.

So she finds herself by a well, in the middle of the day, going to draw water at a time when she would not have to endure the sneers and gossip and cattiness of the other women in her town. She carries her empty jar with her, so symbolic of her empty life; coming day after day after day to the well to try and quench the thirst deep within her. It is an exhausting process, trying to keep your jar full, trying to quench this insatiable thirst. Somehow, no matter how hard you try, it always ends up empty again. So whether dipping her jar in the well of Jacob, or in the well of relationships, nothing has been able to keep her full for very long—if at all. But what else can she do?

So she comes day after day after day. Until she meets Jesus, that is. And when she meets him in the heat of the day, at that very well, he speaks to her in a way that no one had ever spoken to her before, almost as if he understood these inner dynamics. And almost as if he knew the answer to the conundrum of her thirsty soul.

For He spoke of something called *living water*, a mysterious type of water that could satisfy her deepest longings and leave her never being thirsty again. *"Everyone who drinks this water will be thirsty again, but whoever drinks the water I give him will never thirst. Indeed, the water I give him will become in him a spring of water welling up to eternal life,"* he tells her. You see, he was incredibly interested in the quality of her life. He wants fullness for her, he wants joy for her, he wants her deepest longings to be satisfied forever in Him.

And He wants the same for you. Where do you go to quench your thirst? What do you do to try and fill the deepest longings of your soul? What wells do you try and draw from? Do you really believe that God cares about the quality of your life? Do you really believe that He can offer you the fullness and life you were created for? Do you really believe that if you come to Him and drink this living water that you—like the woman—will leave your water jar behind and run off to tell others about the One who knows you better and loves you more than anyone ever can or will?

For Your Journal: What is your heart most thirsty for? What are your deepest longings? Where do you go to

have those longings satisfied? Do you believe that
Jesus can quench the deepest longings of your heart?
For Prayer: Drink in the presence and affection of your
God—the stream of living waters.

Day 21

Theme: Broken Wells
Opening Prayer: O God, giver of life and source of
living water. Forgive me for all the places other than you
that I go to satisfy the deepest longings of my heart.
Help me to see what broken wells I go to each day in
search of the fullness only you can provide. Allow me to
quench the thirsts of my soul in You this day, and in
nothing, or no one, else. Through Christ. Amen.

Read: John 4:13-18
   *Jesus answered, "Everyone who drinks this water will
be thirsty again, but whoever drinks the water I give him
will never thirst. Indeed, the water I give him will become
in him a spring of water welling up to eternal life."*
   *The woman said to him, "Sir, give me this water so
that I won't get thirsty and have to keep coming here to
draw water."*
   He told her, "Go, call your husband and come back."
   "I have no husband," she replied.
   *Jesus said to her, "You are right when you say you
have no husband. The fact is, you have had five
husbands, and the man you now have is not your
husband. What you have just said is quite true."*

Thoughts for Reflection: Trying to satisfy our thirst can
be an incredibly exhausting process—you can hear it in
the Samaritan woman's words, "*so I won't have to keep
coming here to draw water.*" Our hearts seem to be a
bottom-less pit, in constant need of love and affirmation
and significance and value. We just don't seem to be

able to get full and stay that way. We always long for more. It is a never-ending process of filling and filling and refilling—again and again and again. Why? Because ultimately we turn to all the wrong places in our attempt to quench our thirst. Places that were never intended to fill the deepest longings of our souls. Jeremiah says it this way:

> *My people have committed two sins; they have forsaken me, the spring of living water, and have dug their own cisterns [wells], broken cisterns that cannot hold water. (Jeremiah 2:13)*

The woman at this well feels that exhaustion. She has gone to the well of relationship time after time only to watch the initial fullness of her soul leak out of the cracks of her broken heart. Nothing and no one has ever been able to quench the deepest longings of her soul...until now? Could Jesus really offer her what he says? It sounds too good to be true. And it is too good, but it is also too true. In Jesus she has found what she has truly wanted all of her life.

For Your Journal: What are the broken wells you most often run to in an attempt to fulfill the deepest longings of your heart? How well do they work? What would it mean to drink from Jesus?

For Prayer: Sit before God in silence for a few minutes. Ask him to show you your broken wells. Make a list of them. One-by-one give them to God in prayer. Ask him to help you drink from him instead.

Day 22

Theme: Faith

Opening Prayer: O Lord, help me to really believe. Help me to really believe your heart for me is good. Help me to really believe that nothing can separate me from your love. Help me to really believe you will do what you say you will do. Help me to take you at your word. In the name of Jesus. Amen.

Read: John 4:43-54

After the two days he left for Galilee. (Now Jesus himself had pointed out that a prophet has no honor in his own country.) When he arrived in Galilee, the Galileans welcomed him. They had seen all that he had done in Jerusalem at the Passover Feast, for they also had been there.

Once more he visited Cana in Galilee, where he had turned the water into wine. And there was a certain royal official whose son lay sick at Capernaum. When this man heard that Jesus had arrived in Galilee from Judea, he went to him and begged him to come and heal his son, who was close to death.

"Unless you people see miraculous signs and wonders," Jesus told him, "you will never believe."

The royal official said, "Sir, come down before my child dies."

Jesus replied, "You may go. Your son will live." The man took Jesus at his word and departed. While he was still on the way, his servants met him with the news that his boy was living. When he inquired as to the time when his son got better, they said to him, "The fever left him yesterday at the seventh hour."

Then the father realized that this was the exact time at which Jesus had said to him, "Your son will live." So he and all his household believed.

This was the second miraculous sign that Jesus performed, having come from Judea to Galilee.

Thoughts for Reflection: What does the word *faith* mean? Many have tried to define it. The writer of the book of Hebrews says it is "being sure of what we hope for and certain of what we do not see" (Hebrews 11:1). A. W. Tozer says that faith is "the gaze of the soul on a loving God" (*The Pursuit of God*). Martin Luther called faith "the yes of the soul." And Frederick Buechner says that faith is "the direction your feet start moving when you find that you are loved."

But maybe there is no better definition of the word *faith* than the one offered here in the fourth chapter of John. It says the royal official "*took Jesus at his word*." What a great definition of faith. Believing that what God has said is true. Being convinced. Convinced that he loves us the way he says he does. Convinced that he is in control and can be trusted with our lives. Convinced that he will truly care for us and those we love. Convinced.

Is there a place in your life right now where you are having to walk by faith? A place where you are having to believe that God's heart for you is good even though you have a hard time seeing it in the circumstances. What does it mean for you to "take Jesus at his word" right now?

More Thoughts: Faith as it ripens turns into an almost insatiable appetite, and the awake lion must prowl for God in places it once feared."

~John of the Cross

For Your Journal: What is your best picture of faith—draw it or write about it.

For Prayer: Pray about the circumstances in your life or heart that are requiring you to have faith. Ask God to allow you to completely give those things to him.

Day 23

Theme: Do you want to get well?

Opening Prayer: Lord Jesus, help me to want you more than I want anything else. Give me the courage to face your question head on, to leave behind *life on the mat*, to *Get up, pick up my mat and walk,* and truly follow you. Amen.

Read: John 5:1-15

Some time later, Jesus went up to Jerusalem for a feast of the Jews. Now there is in Jerusalem near the Sheep Gate a pool, which in Aramaic is called Bethesda and which is surrounded by five covered colonnades. Here a great number of disabled people used to lie—the blind, the lame, the paralyzed. One who was there had been an invalid for thirty-eight years. When Jesus saw him lying there and learned that he had been in this condition for a long time, he asked him, "Do you want to get well?"

"Sir," the invalid replied, "I have no one to help me into the pool when the water is stirred. While I am trying to get in, someone else goes down ahead of me."

Then Jesus said to him, "Get up! Pick up your mat and walk." At once the man was cured; he picked up his mat and walked.

The day on which this took place was a Sabbath, and so the Jews said to the man who had been healed, "It is the Sabbath; the law forbids you to carry your mat."

But he replied, "The man who made me well said to me, 'Pick up your mat and walk.' "

So they asked him, "Who is this fellow who told you to pick it up and walk?"

The man who was healed had no idea who it was, for Jesus had slipped away into the crowd that was there.

Later Jesus found him at the temple and said to him, "See, you are well again. Stop sinning or something worse may happen to you." The man went away and told the Jews that it was Jesus who had made him well.

Thoughts for Reflection: It seems like a simple enough question that Jesus asks the man at the pool. *"Do you want to get well?"* I mean he had been there for 38 years. You would think it would be easy enough to answer. But there is a lot more to the question than meets the eye.

For thirty-eight years this man had gotten used to a certain way of life—nothing was asked of him, nothing was expected of him, he had no responsibility to anyone. After all, he was an invalid right. That's who he was—

how he defined himself. It's funny how we will grab hold of anything, even if it is negative, if it gives us a sense of identity. And so he was an invalid. Even the word sounds harsh...in-valid...not valid. Not much, but I guess it's better than no identity at all.

Jesus' question cuts right to the heart of his main issue. *"Do you want to get well?"* "Do you want to let go of the way you have seen yourself and defined yourself for most of your life?" "Do you want to be healed and live as a whole person from now on, with all of its beauty and all of its responsibility?" "You better be sure," Jesus seems to be saying, "because I can make you whole again and your life will never be the same. I will totally redefine who you are. Do you want that?"

Do you?

For Your Journal: Do you want to get well?

For Prayer: Ask God to tell you how he sees you—who you really are. Ask Him for the grace and courage to be that person—to find your identity completely in Him.

Day 24

Theme: The Father and the Son

Opening Prayer: Heavenly Father, thank you that through Jesus we are made members of your household—your dearly loved sons and daughters. Help us to live out of that reality each second of each day, so that we may be beautiful reflections of your extravagant love and tender mercy to all those we come into contact with. Through Jesus. Amen.

Read: John 5:16-30

So, because Jesus was doing these things on the Sabbath, the Jews persecuted him. Jesus said to them, "My Father is always at his work to this very day, and I, too, am working." For this reason the Jews tried all the harder to kill him; not only was he breaking the Sabbath, but he was even calling God his own Father, making himself equal with God.

Jesus gave them this answer: "I tell you the truth, the Son can do nothing by himself; he can do only what he sees his Father doing, because whatever the Father does the Son also does. For the Father loves the Son and shows him all he does. Yes, to your amazement he will show him even greater things than these. For just as the Father raises the dead and gives them life, even so the Son gives life to whom he is pleased to give it. Moreover, the Father judges no one, but has entrusted all judgment to the Son, that all may honor the Son just as they honor the Father. He who does not honor the Son does not honor the Father, who sent him.
"I tell you the truth, whoever hears my word and believes him who sent me has eternal life and will not be condemned; he has crossed over from death to life. I tell you the truth, a time is coming and has now come when the dead will hear the voice of the Son of God and those who hear will live. For as the Father has life in himself, so he has granted the Son to have life in himself. And he has given him authority to judge because he is the Son of Man.

"Do not be amazed at this, for a time is coming when all who are in their graves will hear his voice and come out—those who have done good will rise to live, and those who have done evil will rise to be condemned. By myself I can do nothing; I judge only as I hear, and my judgment is just, for I seek not to please myself but him who sent me.

Thoughts for Reflection: The question the Jewish leaders ask the man at the pool is: "Who is this fellow that told you to pick it up and walk?" Who is this Jesus? It is a question lots of people (including the disciples) are asking. So Jesus answers—with his first long discourse of John's gospel. You can tell by the length of his answer that he considers the question very important, as should we.

His answer focuses mainly on the unique nature of his relationship with God and the intimate connection that exists between the two—similar to that described in the first few verses of chapter one. His main description of this relationship is that of a father and son—a picture that makes the Jewish leaders incredibly uncomfortable. No God-fearing Jew would ever have had the courage to call the Almighty God his father. As a matter of fact Jews would not even say (or fully spell) the name of God (Yahweh) much less refer to Him in such familiar terms.

But Jesus is on a mission—a mission to bring God near. He has come to offer all of us a much more intimate picture of the God we thought was so distant and uninvolved. A picture of a God who can't keep his hands off his creation, but longs to speak to them, to touch them, to fill them with life. One in which Yahweh (the name by which God revealed himself to Moses in Exodus 3) is pictured as a heavenly father and Jesus as His tenderly loved Son. And as God's Son, it is He who can offer us entry into the divine life—the divine family. All we must do is believe…be fully persuaded. Are you?

For Your Journal: How does Jesus' relationship with his Father make you feel? What kind of hope does it give you? Do you see yourself as God's beloved son or daughter?

For Prayer: Pray that Jesus would give you eyes to see yourself as God sees you. Sit and enjoy the fact that you are Abba's child through Christ.

Day 25

Theme: Testimony about Jesus

Opening Prayer: Lord Jesus, thank you that all things give testimony to you and your goodness. Help us to have hearts to listen to that testimony this day, that we would be more and more convinced of its truth—to the core of our being. Amen.

Read: John 5:31-47

"If I testify about myself, my testimony is not valid. There is another who testifies in my favor, and I know that his testimony about me is valid.

"You have sent to John and he has testified to the truth. Not that I accept human testimony; but I mention it that you may be saved. John was a lamp that burned and gave light, and you chose for a time to enjoy his light.

"I have testimony weightier than that of John. For the very work that the Father has given me to finish, and which I am doing, testifies that the Father has sent me. And the Father who sent me has himself testified concerning me. You have never heard his voice nor seen his form, nor does his word dwell in you, for you do not believe the one he sent. You diligently study the Scriptures because you think that by them you possess eternal life. These are the Scriptures that testify about me, yet you refuse to come to me to have life.

"I do not accept praise from men, but I know you. I know that you do not have the love of God in your hearts. I have come in my Father's name, and you do not accept me; but if someone else comes in his own name, you will accept him. How can you believe if you accept praise from one another, yet make no effort to obtain the praise that comes from the only God?

"But do not think I will accuse you before the Father. Your accuser is Moses, on whom your hopes are set. If you believed Moses, you would believe me, for he wrote about me. But since you do not believe what he wrote, how are you going to believe what I say?"

Thoughts for Reflection: Testimony. It is simply telling what you know to be true. The Jews wanted witnesses that would validate the claims of Jesus—that he was God's son. Validation in a court of law, however, required the agreement of two witnesses. Who would come forth and testify on Jesus' behalf—who would come forth and tell the world who he really was?

Jesus steps into the courtroom and begins to call his witnesses to the stand. First witness, John the Baptist. John said that Jesus was "the Lamb of God who takes away the sin of the world (John 1:29)." Every good Jew knew that picture very well, and they knew that God was the only one who could forgive sin. Jesus, being the Lamb of God, is the means through which God would forgive that sin, so in essence John was saying that Jesus was equal to God. Not a bad start.

The next witness to take the stand is God the Father himself. It was at the baptism of Jesus where the Father said in a loud voice (from the heavens), "This is my Son, whom I love; with him I am well pleased (Matthew 3:17)." Hard to argue with that.

Jesus continues to build his case. The next two witnesses really hit the Jews where they live. The third testimony Jesus calls on is the Scripture, the very word of God. The Jews prided themselves in knowing this one backwards and forward. They would have known the large number of places in the Law and Prophets that talk about the Messiah to come—such as *"But you, Bethlehem, in the land of Judah; are by no means least among the rulers of Judah; for out of you will come a ruler who will be the shepherd of my people Israel* (Micah 5:2)." Jesus asserts that words such as these in the Scriptures refer to him.

The final witness is Moses, the ultimate Israelite— every Jew's hero. Even he wrote about Jesus—from beginning to end—starting with Genesis 3:15 (after the fall of Adam and Eve in the garden) when God said, *"And I will put an enmity between you and the woman [talking to the serpent], and between your offspring and hers; he will crush your head, and you will strike his heel."* Another crushing blow to the prosecution (the Jews).

The defense rests. The list of witnesses is impressive. Now it is up to those who have heard the testimony to decide what they will believe. All have provided the same testimony—that Jesus is the Son of

God, the Messiah, the Christ. Now the evidence is in your hands. What say you?

More Thoughts:

He [Jesus] is the image of the invisible God, the firstborn over all creation. For by him all things were created: things in heaven and on earth, visible and invisible, whether thrones or powers or rulers or authorities; all things were created by him and for him. He is before all things, and in him all things hold together. And he is the head of his body, the church; he is the beginning and the firstborn from among the dead, so that in everything he might have the supremacy. For God was pleased to have all his fullness dwell in him...

~Colossians 1:15-19

For Your Journal: What is your testimony about Jesus? Who is he to you? What has he done in your life thus far?

For Prayer: Tell God why you believe in Him. Tell him about all the things you appreciate about him. Thank him for the evidence of his involvement in your life. Ask him to lead you to others who need to hear your story (testimony).

Day 26

Theme: Multiplying the meager

Opening Prayer: Heavenly Father, take my meager offerings—my gifts and efforts and dreams—and multiply them for your kingdom; that thousands may be fed by my little brown bag through the power of your Spirit and in the name of your Son Jesus. Amen.

Read: John 6:1-15

Some time after this, Jesus crossed to the far shore of the Sea of Galilee (that is, the Sea of Tiberias), and a great crowd of people followed him because they saw the miraculous signs he had performed on the sick.

Then Jesus went up on a mountainside and sat down with his disciples. The Jewish Passover Feast was near.

When Jesus looked up and saw a great crowd coming toward him, he said to Philip, "Where shall we buy bread for these people to eat?" He asked this only to test him, for he already had in mind what he was going to do.

Philip answered him, "Eight months' wages would not buy enough bread for each one to have a bite!"

Another of his disciples, Andrew, Simon Peter's brother, spoke up, "Here is a boy with five small barley loaves and two small fish, but how far will they go among so many?"

Jesus said, "Have the people sit down." There was plenty of grass in that place, and the men sat down, about five thousand of them.

Jesus then took the loaves, gave thanks, and distributed to those who were seated as much as they wanted. He did the same with the fish.

When they had all had enough to eat, he said to his disciples, "Gather the pieces that are left over. Let nothing be wasted." So they gathered them and filled twelve baskets with the pieces of the five barley loaves left over by those who had eaten.

After the people saw the miraculous sign that Jesus did, they began to say, "Surely this is the Prophet who is to come into the world." Jesus, knowing that they intended to come and make him king by force, withdrew again to a mountain by himself.

Thoughts for Reflection: The crowds were growing; they seemed to follow Jesus everywhere he went. They just couldn't get enough of him; the signs he performed on the sick were simply miraculous. On this particular day they followed him around the Sea of Galilee and up on a mountainside. The day was quickly drawing to a close and they were far from anywhere to get anything to eat.

Jesus surveys the scene and senses an opportunity to teach his disciples a valuable lesson about God's provision. He asks Phillip where they might find bread to feed the rapidly growing crowd. Phillip and his disciple-buddies begin to scramble for options, but all the scramble produces is a little boy with five *small* barley loaves and two *small* fish—hardly enough to feed thousands of people.

Jesus tells the disciples to get the people into groups and have them sit down. He then looks to the Father and gives thanks; distributing the food to all who were hungry. And everybody eats and eats and eats…until they have all had enough.

He then sends the disciples out to gather the leftovers and— wouldn't you know it—twelve basketfuls are left over: one for each of the disciples…simply amazing! Not only had Jesus provided abundantly for all of the crowds of people, but he had also provided exactly enough for the disciples as well. All this from a little boy's sack lunch—five *small* barley loaves and two *small* fish.

The moral of the story is: He provides! He takes the meager and multiplies it…with food…and with life.

For Your Journal: What in your life or heart do you desire Jesus to take and multiply? Where are you needing to trust God for his provision? What part of your life feels like leftovers, but could be used by God to feed your soul?

For Prayer: Ask God what things in your life he desires you to give him so he might multiply it to feed many. Listen carefully for his response—write it down.

Day 27

Theme: Calm in the storm

Opening Prayer: Lord Jesus, when the sea of life grows rough and I am tempted to let fear overcome me, allow me to hear your voice saying, "It is I; don't be afraid." And let those words calm the waters of my heart and soul, giving me the peace that only trusting you can bring.

Read: John 6:16-24

When evening came, his disciples went down to the lake, where they got into a boat and set off across the lake for Capernaum. By now it was dark, and Jesus had not yet joined them. A strong wind was blowing and the waters grew rough. When they had rowed three or three and a half miles they saw Jesus approaching the boat, walking on the water; and they were terrified. But he said to them, "It is I; don't be afraid." Then they were willing to take him into the boat, and immediately the boat reached the shore where they were heading.

The next day the crowd that had stayed on the opposite shore of the lake realized that only one boat had been there, and that Jesus had not entered it with his disciples, but that they had gone away alone. Then some boats from Tiberias landed near the place where the people had eaten the bread after the Lord had given thanks. Once the crowd realized that neither Jesus nor his disciples were there, they got into the boats and went to Capernaum in search of Jesus.

Thoughts for Reflection: Before meeting the disciples on the boat, Jesus is alone on the mountain. He walks down slowly— grinning after listening to affectionate words from his father and soaking up the stillness after a day crowded with people and noise. His eyes sparkle as God stirs the wind and sprinkles refreshing drops of rain onto his face through the evergreen boughs. Jesus probably loves walking on the water the way I love walking on the beach in a storm. The fury of the wind and water careen ecstatically about, but he doesn't feel scared, just exhilarated by nature swirling through the air and at his feet. He is dancing in the waves while the disciples cower in fear. Peter senses this wild peace as Jesus approaches:

"Don't be afraid," Jesus laughs
as he sees the stricken faces
and hears a barely audible
whisper, "It's a ghost—"
from the quaking boat.
"It's only me."

Peter, scared as the rest
but intrigued by the peace
in the Voice
stutters through fear,
"Jesus, if it's really you,

ask me to come dance on the water."

"Come,
dance with me," answers Jesus.

So Peter steps off the boat
onto the whirling, raging dance floor.
He looks into Jesus' eyes,
letting him lead the first steps
on the water,
and, for a few miraculous moments,

they dance.

Amazed at the wildness of the dance,
Peter looks away just as the
sea and sky and fish
dance more fiercely to welcome
him to the revelry.

Fear grips him as
he begins to sink,
realizing his feet
are anchored on nothing
but mystery,
moving to a rhythm
he doesn't yet understand—

though nature seems to know
the same song
that coursed through him
in the beginning,

which frightens and excites
him all the more.

"Lord, save me!" he cries
and looks up to find the playful eyes
of the One he has come to love
but not understand.

"Why did you doubt?" Jesus smiles
as he reaches down for Peter's frigid hand
and pulls him gently into the boat.

"We could have danced all night."

The storm slows its dance to the
rhythm of waves lapping a lullaby
against the small boat.
Disciples look in awe
on the peaceful, smiling One
and their friend
who is beginning to never recover
from a taste of the dance.

"Truly you are the Son of God," they mutter.

"No one else could dance like that . . ."
(*Storm Dance* by Caroline McKinney Karnes)
For Your Journal: What are the storms in your life right now? What are the things that are causing upheaval or turmoil? Where do you think God is in the midst of this storm? How might he desire to offer you peace?
For Prayer: Place the storms of your life before God; be ruthlessly honest about what they are and how you feel about them. Ask for his words of peace and calm in the midst of the struggle. Allow him to comfort you and care

for your heart. Pray also for the storms of others around you and for His peace to come to them as well.

Day 28

Theme: Bread of Life

Opening Prayer: O Bread of Life, satisfy the deepest hunger of my soul this day with the nourishment of your Spirit. Allow me to feed on you, that I might have true life. Keep me from feeding at the table of the world and trying to fill my heart with that which was never designed to offer fullness or life. In the name of Jesus I pray. Amen.

Read: John 6:25-59

When they found him on the other side of the lake, they asked him, "Rabbi, when did you get here?"

Jesus answered, "I tell you the truth, you are looking for me, not because you saw miraculous signs but because you ate the loaves and had your fill. Do not work for food that spoils, but for food that endures to eternal life, which the Son of Man will give you. On him God the Father has placed his seal of approval."

Then they asked him, "What must we do to do the works God requires?"

Jesus answered, "The work of God is this: to believe in the one he has sent."

So they asked him, "What miraculous sign then will you give that we may see it and believe you? What will you do? Our forefathers ate the manna in the desert; as it is written: 'He gave them bread from heaven to eat.'"

Jesus said to them, "I tell you the truth, it is not Moses who has given you the bread from heaven, but it is my Father who gives you the true bread from heaven. For the bread of God is he who comes down from heaven and gives life to the world."

"Sir," they said, "from now on give us this bread."

Then Jesus declared, "I am the bread of life. He who comes to me will never go hungry, and he who believes in me will never be thirsty. But as I told you, you have seen me and still you do not believe. All that the Father gives me will come to me, and whoever comes to me I will never drive away. For I have come down from heaven not to do my will but to do the will of him who sent me. And this is the will of him who sent me, that I shall lose none of all that he has given me, but raise them up at the last day. For my Father's will is that everyone who looks to the Son and believes in him shall have eternal life, and I will raise him up at the last day."

At this the Jews began to grumble about him because he said, "I am the bread that came down from heaven." They said, "Is this not Jesus, the son of Joseph, whose father and mother we know? How can he now say, 'I came down from heaven'?"

"Stop grumbling among yourselves," Jesus answered. "No one can come to me unless the Father who sent me draws him, and I will raise him up at the last day. It is written in the Prophets: 'They will all be taught by God.' Everyone who listens to the Father and learns from him comes to me. No one has seen the Father except the one who is from God; only he has seen the Father. I tell you the truth, he who believes has everlasting life. I am the bread of life. Your forefathers ate the manna in the desert, yet they died. But here is the bread that comes down from heaven, which a man may eat and not die. I am the living bread that came down from heaven. If anyone eats of this bread, he will live forever. This bread is my flesh, which I will give for the life of the world."

Then the Jews began to argue sharply among themselves, "How can this man give us his flesh to eat?"

Jesus said to them, "I tell you the truth, unless you eat the flesh of the Son of Man and drink his blood, you have no life in you. Whoever eats my flesh and drinks my blood has eternal life, and I will raise him up at the last day. For my flesh is real food and my blood is real drink. Whoever eats my flesh and drinks my blood remains in me, and I in him. Just as the living Father sent me and I live because of the Father, so the one who feeds on me will live because of me. This is the bread that came down from heaven. Your forefathers ate manna and died, but he who feeds on this bread will live forever." He said this while teaching in the synagogue in Capernaum.

Thoughts for Reflection: In the wilderness the children of Israel grumbled against Moses and Aaron—and ultimately God—because they were hungry and could find nothing to eat (Exodus 16). They even went so far as to wish they were slaves again, complaining that at least when they were held captive in Egypt they had food to eat. It is amazing what a little discontent can do to your mind, heart, and soul as it snowballs rapidly downhill and makes us totally lose perspective.

Well God heard the grumbling of the Israelites and did something totally amazing. He actually rained down bread from heaven. Each morning they would wake up and there would be something (bread) covering the ground called manna—which means "what is it?" Every day for forty years God rained this manna down from heaven, and the Israelites gathered it each day and ate until they were satisfied. Thus, God fed his people.

That is the backstory for what we find here in John 6. God, once again, is telling the children of Israel that He is going to provide bread from heaven for them to eat. Only this time the bread is not going to be called manna, this bread is called Jesus. It was not physical bread to nourish the body, but spiritual bread to nourish the heart, soul, and spirit. God was inviting his people to feed on Him in their hearts by faith.

"I am the bread of life. Your forefathers ate the manna in the desert, yet they died. But here is the bread that comes down from heaven, which a man may eat and not die. I am the living bread that came down from heaven. If anyone eats of this bread, he will live forever," said Jesus. In this life we can try and feed on many different things—affirmation, achievement, success, popularity, performance, appearance—but these things can never fill us. In fact, if we try to feed on that type of bread we will eventually die of starvation. Feeding on

Jesus is the only way to true and lasting life..."*he who feeds on this bread will live forever."*
For your Journal: What are the typical things you try to feed your soul with? How well does it fill you? What is the biggest obstacle to your feeding on Jesus? What does it mean to feed on Jesus?
For Prayer: Ask God to show you where your soul feeds most. Ask him to show you what it means to feed your soul on Him alone. Ask him to give you a deep hunger for Him and His Word.

Day 29

Theme: You don't want to leave too, do you?
Opening Prayer: You called, You cried, you shattered my deafness. You sparkled, you blazed, You drove away my blindness. You shed your fragrance, and I drew in my breath, and I pant for You. I tasted and now I hunger and thirst. You touched me, and now I burn with longing for your peace.
~ St. Augustine

Read: John 6:60-71
On hearing it, many of his disciples said, "This is a hard teaching. Who can accept it?"
Aware that his disciples were grumbling about this, Jesus said to them, "Does this offend you? What if you see the Son of Man ascend to where he was before! The Spirit gives life; the flesh counts for nothing. The words I have spoken to you are spirit and they are life. Yet there are some of you who do not believe." For Jesus had known from the beginning which of them did not believe and who would betray him. He went on to say, "This is why I told you that no one can come to me unless the Father has enabled him."
From this time many of his disciples turned back and no longer followed him.
"You do not want to leave too, do you?" Jesus asked

the Twelve.

Simon Peter answered him, "Lord, to whom shall we go? You have the words of eternal life. We believe and know that you are the Holy One of God."

Then Jesus replied, "Have I not chosen you, the Twelve? Yet one of you is a devil!" (He meant Judas, the son of Simon Iscariot, who, though one of the Twelve, was later to betray him.)

Thoughts for Reflection: What a key moment it is for Jesus' young band of disciples. He had just been talking to the crowds about how if they attempt to draw life from any source other than him, they are actually feeding on death itself. It is a hard truth to hear. Some even imagine he is speaking in terms of physical reality rather than spiritual reality.

Slowly, many of his followers leave and go back to their former ways of life. The disciples are at a crossroads, what will they do? Will they stick around to see if they can understand what these strange words mean? To feed on him? Or will they leave? Where will they go for life? To Jesus? Or to the things they had pursued up to the point that they met him?

Jesus asks them a pointed question. "You do not want to leave too, do you?"

Peter, as usual, is the first to answer. And his answer is beautiful: "To whom shall we go?" Where else is there? "You have the words of eternal life." We will stay and figure out what it means to feed on you.

Another great question asked by Jesus. And one definitely worth considering ourselves. Where will you go for life? "You don't want to leave too, do you?" Even if all your friends do? Will you stay? Will you allow Me to satisfy your soul with the richest of fare (Isaiah 55:2)?
More Thoughts:
Come, all you who are thirsty, come to the waters;
and you who have no money, come, buy and eat!
Why spend money on what is not bread,
and your labor on what does not satisfy?
Listen, listen to me, and eat what is good

and your soul will delight in the richest of fare.

~Isaiah 55:1-2

For Your Journal: What does it mean for you to feed on God? To trust completely in Jesus as your only source of life? Are you willing to do that?

For Prayer: Answer Jesus as he asks, "You don't want to leave too, do you?"

Day 30

Theme: The right time

Opening Prayer: O God, Eternal Father, help me to see all of life as you see it, so that I will be able to discern between what is really important from what is merely urgent. Give me your concept of time, that I may walk at your pace rather than my own. In the name of Jesus. Amen.

Read: John 7:1-9

After this, Jesus went around in Galilee, purposely staying away from Judea because the Jews there were waiting to take his life. But when the Jewish Feast of Tabernacles was near, Jesus' brothers said to him, "You ought to leave here and go to Judea, so that your disciples may see the miracles you do. No one who wants to become a public figure acts in secret. Since you are doing these things, show yourself to the world." For even his own brothers did not believe in him.

Therefore Jesus told them, "The right time for me has not yet come; for you any time is right. The world cannot hate you, but it hates me because I testify that what it does is evil. You go to the Feast. I am not yet going up to this Feast, because for me the right time has not yet come." Having said this, he stayed in Galilee.

Thoughts for Reflection: They say timing is everything. Well, that certainly seems to be true about Jesus.

People were always pressing him; pushing for him to go here or there, or to do this or that. But Jesus operated by a different clock than most of us operate by. He was not so much concerned about chronological time as he was about the *right time*. The *right time* is God's time—the fullness of time. It is time that is ripe for something to happen. It is time with a capital T.

Even Jesus' family had an agenda for him, pressing him to do certain things at certain times. But Jesus would not allow even this to sway him; he was in tune with a heavenly clock that allowed him to know when the time was *right*. He moved at a different pace, not the pace of the world, but the pace of his Father.

What about you? What determines the pace at which you live your life? What determines the things you do in a day and the way you set your priorities? What determines whether or not the way you manage your time is *right*?

For Your Journal: Where do you spend most of your time? What does that say about what your life is centered on? What determines the pace of your life? Where you spend your time? How can you live life more centered on God's time?

For Prayer: Hold your life before God in prayer and ask Him to give you insight into how he might want you to spend your days and hours.

Continuing On: Now that our thirty days have drawn to a close, hopefully you have begun to sense the rhythm of what your time with God can be like. Now continue on. Below is a reading guide for the rest of the book of John. After you have finished it, seek out a godly man or woman to give you some suggestions on where to go from here.

If this structure has provided a fruitful space for you to be with God, you might want to try one of the following books next: *Disciplines for the Inner Life* by Bob Benson and Michael W. Benson, *A Guide to Prayer for All Who Seek God* by Rueben P. Job and Norman Shawchuck, or get a copy of my book *Reflections* (a journey through the gospel of Mark), or the *Blue Book*. Whatever you do, know that God deeply desires to be with you and to continue forming and molding your heart and soul into the image of His Son Jesus.

Day 31- John 7:10-24
Day 32- John 7:25-44
Day 33- John 7:45-52
Day 34- John 8:1-11
Day 35- John 8:12-30
Day 36- John 8:31-41
Day 37- John 8:42-47
Day 38- John 8:48-59
Day 39- John 9:1-34
Day 40- John 9:35-41
Day 41- John 10:1-21
Day 42- John 10:22-42
Day 43- John 11:1-44
Day 44- John 11:45-57
Day 45- John 12:1-11
Day 46- John 12:12-19
Day 47- John 12:20-36
Day 48- John 12:37-50
Day 49- John 13:1-17
Day 50- John 13:18-30

Day 51- John 13:31-38
Day 52- John 14:1-4
Day 53- John 14:5-14
Day 54- John 14:15-24
Day 55- John 14:25-31
Day 56- John 15:1-17
Day 57- John 15:18-27
Day 58- John 16:1-4
Day 59- John 16:5-16
Day 60- John 16:17-33
Day 61- John 17:1-5
Day 62- John 17:6-19
Day 63- John 17:20-26
Day 64- John 18:1-11
Day 65- John 18:12-27
Day 66- John 18:28-40
Day 67- John 19:1-16
Day 68- John 19:17-27
Day 69- John 19:28-37
Day 70- John 19:38-42
Day 71- John 20:1-9
Day 72- John 20:10-18
Day 73- John 20:19-31
Day 74- John 21:1-14
Day 75- John 21:15-25

Made in the USA
San Bernardino, CA
05 December 2016